The
KINGMAKERS

How the Media Threatens
Our Security and Our Democracy

Senator Mike Gravel
AND DAVID EISENBACH, PhD

ISBN-10: 1-59777-586-X
ISBN-13: 978-1-59777-586-1

Library of Congress Cataloging-In-Publication Data Available

Book Design by: Carolyn Wendt

Cover Photography: Keith Olberman, Paul Drinkwater/NBC NewsWire via
AP Images; Bill O'Reilly, AP Images/Jeff Christensen: Brian Williams, AP Images/
Reed Saxon; Chris Matthews, AP Images/Mark J. Terrill; Katie Couric, AP Images/
Lucas Jackson; Tim Russert, AP Images/Jim Cole; Anderson Cooper, AP Images/
Diane Bondareff; Wolf Blitzer, AP Images/Jae C. Hong

Printed in the United States of America

Phoenix Books, Inc.
9465 Wilshire Boulevard, Suite 840
Beverly Hills, CA 90212

10 9 8 7 6 5 4 3 2 1

Dedicated to
Whitney Gravel and Stephanie Gangi

CONTENTS

INTRODUCTION

Ever wonder why all the big news organizations report the same things even when they're inaccurate? It would make sense that various news outlets would report the same stories if they were true. But why are news reports from all the main media outlets so consistently and similarly wrong? The answer is revealed in this look at the news coverage of the main issues over the past several years: 9/11, Iraq, Iran, and the 2008 election.

This investigation began with conversations I had with my co-author Dr. David Eisenbach, a media specialist at Columbia University. He and I were both baffled by the glaring discrepancy between reality and what the media presents as "news." After some discussion and research, we came up with an answer.

There is no vast media conspiracy to deceive the American public. The glaring discrepancy between reality and our news coverage is the product of the systemic flaw in how news is generated. Journalists, editors, and news producers do not just collect and relay facts, they also fit them into a storyline. A storyline emerges when the media first starts reporting on an event. On the 9/11 attack, Iraq, and Iran, the Bush Administration created the storylines that the media echoed. Facts or claims that supported the general storylines were featured in the news coverage while anything that deviated from the storylines got dropped or downplayed.

Once a storyline gets adopted, the media becomes an echo chamber repeating the same inaccurate and dangerous claims over and over. The media echoed the Bush Administration's charges about Iraqi and Iranian WMD programs that did not exist. They allowed a neo-con clique to push the United States into an unnecessary war with Iraq and almost with Iran. The Iraq War has shattered the lives of tens of thousands of Americans, and a war with Iran would have been even more devastating. The failure of our media to present the public with accurate views of our world and its leaders poses a greater threat to our national security and American lives than terrorism.

The media echo chamber also undermines our democracy by adopting storylines that favor certain candidates over others. Long before the majority of voters paid attention to the election, the media filtered the presidential field and chose the "leading candidates." The greatest threat to our democracy is not money—It's the media.

Our book is not a lament or a finger-pointing screed. It's a call to action. America has a choice. We can believe the inaccurate storylines while we watch our kids die in needless wars and surrender our democracy to a lazy media elite. Or we can educate ourselves about how the media echo chamber operates so we don't get fooled again.

Senator Mike Gravel

CHAPTER ONE

THE REAL 9/11 COVER-UP

"They hate us, because we're free."
George W. Bush, April 2002

9/11 on TV

On September 11, 2001, millions of us sat glued to our TVs watching our fellow citizens suffer, die, and exhibit extraordinary acts of heroism. Never before had so many Americans simultaneously watched a single event unfold in real time. While New Yorkers and Washingtonians saw and smelled the smoke rising from their hometowns, the rest of America and much of the world experienced the trauma and the heroism through the power of television.

This collective trauma was different from Pearl Harbor or the Kennedy assassination. Most of the victims were ordinary people, not leaders or military servicemen who knowingly placed themselves in a life-threatening position in order to serve their country. The 9/11 victims were people who got up that morning and went to work like everyone else. Now we saw our fellow office workers looking out from broken windows, facing the choice between being consumed by flames or plunging 100 stories. We saw a man and woman, two coworkers or perhaps strangers, fatefully join hands and leap.

For days, Americans watched similar scenes replayed by an equally stunned media. It was hard to believe that anything could be normal again. How could we return to our "me first" individualism when we heard nonstop reports of the selfless heroism of the first responders? And how could TV go back to the usual fare of sitcoms and celebrity news after viewers took such a sustained dose of brutal reality? We were told "9/11 changed everything." In the weeks after that horrible morning, no one disagreed.

Though it might have changed everything, images alone can't get people to think and reevaluate. Images can shock, but for them to have an intellectual impact, they need context and explanation. On that morning, we all wanted a leader to explain what was happening and to assure us that he was going to hunt down everyone responsible. We also wanted him to tell us how we could help defend our country. In the hours after the attack, millions of people waited for their president to appear on their TVs and help them make sense of it all.

Our Pet Goat

At 8:48 a.m. on the morning of September 11, 2001, television news programs began broadcasting the first images of the burning World Trade Center. News anchors, reporters, and viewers had little idea what was happening in lower Manhattan, but our government already knew. By that time, the gravity of the situation was clear to the Federal Aviation Administration, the North American Aerospace Defense Command, the National Military Command Center, the Pentagon, the White House, the Secret Service, and Canada's Strategic Command. Thousands of officials in the U.S. and Canadian governments knew three commercial jets had been hijacked: one of them was flown into the World Trade Center's North Tower, a second plane was wildly off course speeding toward Manhattan, and a third plane had abruptly turned around over Ohio and was aimed directly at Washington, D.C. George Bush, however, proceeded with a photo-op at an elementary school in Sarasota to promote "No Child Left Behind."

While our fellow Americans plunged to the sidewalks of lower Manhattan, Bush sat with a collection of children listening to a reading of *My Pet Goat.* When Chief of Staff Andrew Card whispered into his ear that another plane had hit the other tower, Bush flinched but remained seated for seven minutes with a dumbfounded look on his face. Later his spokespeople explained that he wanted to avoid upsetting the kids, but that incredibly lame excuse for his paralysis was betrayed by subsequent events. Bush hung around the school for a whole hour after the first jet hit the World Trade Center and then hop-scotched on Air Force One from a military base in Louisiana to another base in Omaha, briefly appearing before the cameras to deliver two shaky, scripted performances and then disappearing for hours.

Rather than express dismay with our AWOL president, the press simply looked the other way and found their take-charge hero that afternoon in Rudy Giuliani. Giuliani's calm demeanor and unscripted assessments earned him the title of "America's Mayor." But Giuliani wasn't the Commander in Chief.

Cheerleader in Chief

When Bush finally made it back to Washington that evening, the press gave him a pass. Instead of making him the pet goat of 9/11, the media applauded his squinty-eyed pronouncements: "I want justice. There's an old poster out West, as I recall, that said, 'Wanted: Dead or Alive'"; "I'm not going to fire a two-million-dollar missile at a ten-dollar empty tent and hit a camel in the butt. It's going to be decisive"; and "[...] In Western terms, to smoke them out of their caves, to get them running so we can get them." When Bush made it to Ground Zero three days later, he was full of cocksure swagger, grabbing a bullhorn and addressing the rescue workers from atop a fire truck. Clearly his cheerleading days at Yale paid off. The media finally got their images, however belated, of the take-charge Commander in Chief. Like a Hollywood movie, the hero rode into town just in time.

They Hate Us because We're Free

On the first day of the attack on Afghanistan in October 2001, Al Jazeera broadcast a video featuring Osama bin Laden and his deputy, Ayman al-Zawahiri, posing a valid question, "American people, can you ask yourselves why there is so much hate against America?" The answer was obvious to anyone who occasionally read a newspaper or watched the nightly news. For decades the U.S. had been a force for misery in the Middle East.

▶ In 1953, the CIA overthrew Iran's democratically elected secular leader Mossedeq in order to prevent him from taking over the oil interests of powerful multinational companies. The U.S. replaced Iran's democratic government with the authoritarian Shah and trained his secret police, SAVAK, which terrorized the Iranian people for decades.

▶ The U.S. defends repressive regimes of the Persian Gulf oil states, which use their vast wealth to enrich a select few while the majority of their people live in poverty.

▶ The U.S. has blindly supported Israel without care for the millions of Palestinians sitting in refugee camps.

▶ After the first Gulf War, the U.S. enforced sanctions on Iraq that resulted in the deaths of 500,000 children.

The list goes on.

In the week after 9/11, Americans were in search of the answer to the simple question: Why did they attack us? If the media suggested that the U.S. may have contributed to the hatred behind the 9/11 attack, the public might have supported a change of course from our oil-based Middle East policy and constant catering to the Israeli right-wing. Instead, the media went along with George Bush's explanation for 9/11 offered during a September 20, 2001, address to Congress: "Americans are asking, 'Why do they hate us?' They hate what they see right here in this chamber: a democratically elected government. Their leaders are self-appointed. They hate our freedoms: our freedom of religion, our freedom of speech, our freedom to vote and assemble and disagree with each other."

Over the subsequent weeks, the media's talking heads repeated variations of the line "they hate us because we're free." This storyline transmitted several comforting messages: don't worry, don't change a thing, the reason why they hate us is because we're so good and free, keep driving those SUVs, we're number one, and forget the dead Iraqi kids and the Palestinians because we're the best.

But are we the best? Many other countries are free, and they didn't get attacked. Some of those other free countries might be freer than us. The Dutch are free to do drugs. The French can engage in prostitution. Gays in Britain and Israel can serve openly in the military. In just about every country on earth, Janet Jackson's "wardrobe malfunction" is considered entertainment, while in America, it's grounds for a federal investigation and a $550,000 fine. The talking heads in the mainstream media didn't explore these contradictions. They simply swallowed and regurgitated Bush's "they hate us because we're free" applause line and made it their storyline.

Bush then used variations of this line in speeches given around the country in the spring of 2002. "They hate us, because we're free. They hate the thought that Americans welcome all religions. They can't stand that thought. They hate the thought that we educate everybody. They hate our freedoms. They hate the fact that we hold each individual—we dignify each individual. We believe in the dignity of every person. They can't stand that."[1]

A pattern emerged that would be repeated over the next six years. Bush would make a simplistic and dramatic statement. The media would repeat variations of it and Bush would echo variations of the media's variations of his original statement. On the question of why 9/11 happened, the American media served as an echo chamber for George Bush's easy, self-congratulating explanation, however simplistic and inaccurate.

"What is Expected of Us?"

When Bush spoke to a special session of Congress nine days after 9/11, Americans were primed to hear what sacrifices they could make to keep their country safe. Bush had an opportunity to challenge Americans to make themselves and their country better or at least reduce their oil consumption. Instead, he let them off the hook, "Americans are asking, 'What is expected of us?' I ask you to live your lives and hug your children.... I ask you to continue to support the victims of this tragedy with your contributions.... I ask your continued participation and confidence in the American economy.... And finally, please continue praying for the victims of terror and their families, for those in uniform and for our great country."

So what did George Bush ask his fellow Americans to do for their country? Hug, donate, shop, and pray—a bunch of pleasant, painless tasks that would do absolutely nothing to avoid another attack. One might expect someone, anyone, in the mainstream media to point out the absurdity of Bush's call for more hugs and prayers. However, Americans wanted a hero, and the media was determined to give them one—even if Bush wasn't really up to the role.

David Border: "Echoes of Abe Lincoln"

Prior to 9/11, the media dismissed Bush as a lightweight. *U.S. News & World Report* asserted that many Americans saw him as "an affable Texan backslapping his way through a benign era or an untested, fortunate son of a former president." *The Boston Globe* cited *Saturday Night Live's* parody of Bush as "an overgrown boy, eager to please but befuddled as he burrowed about in his brain for a single cogent thought." Even *People* magazine said that prior to 9/11, Bush seemed "poised to become his own Dan Quayle, a White House puppy frisking among the grown-ups."[2] After 9/11, Americans didn't want to see their president as the new Dan Quayle, so the media adopted a new storyline.

The media echo chamber universally acclaimed Bush's speech before Congress. Even wizened Beltway journalist David Broder, the so-called "Dean of the Washington Press Corps," joined the chorus praising the speech. In a *Washington Post* column titled "Echoes of Lincoln," Broder compared Bush to the Great Emancipator: "The powerful but simple words in which the 16th president framed the issues of the Civil War have been the model for the forty-third president's depiction of the struggle that divides the civilized world and the terrorist cabals."

Broder was somehow impressed that, like Lincoln, Bush "tried to make it clear we are not warring on other peoples—not Muslims, not Arabs—but rather on those who threaten the safety of the Union and our God-given freedoms." So Bush should get credit for saying we shouldn't indiscriminately attack all Arabs?

Broder then compared Bush to Lincoln and Kennedy who "came to the presidency after brief and less-than-notable careers in public office.... But each responded to the forces threatening the citadel of freedom in their own times." Lincoln's Civil War leadership saved the Union, and during the Cuban Missile Crisis, Kennedy's cool head saved the world. What exactly did George Bush do to deserve a place in such lofty company? He gave a speech asking Americans to make no sacrifices and shop more. In September 2001, David Broder chucked his journalistic objectivity and drank the Bush Kool-Aid.

The Administration apparently picked up on Border's Lincoln analogy. The White House press corps had never seen Bush with a book, but suddenly he was spotted carrying around a book about Lincoln, *April 1865: The Month That Saved America*. NBC took the bait and invited *April 1865*'s author Jay Winik to appear on the *Today Show* where the historian dutifully declared, "I really think there are certain echoes of Lincoln in [Bush]."[3]

America's Winston Churchill

Soon the media was comparing Bush to other historical figures: Harry Truman (*Washington Post, Fortune, Los Angeles Times*), FDR (*CBS Sunday Morning*), Ronald Reagan (*Fortune*), and Winston Churchill (*Time, U.S. News & World Report*). *Newsweek* observed that when Bush visited London, he spent thirty minutes "sitting in Churchill's chair and admiring the charts and maps." *Time* noted, "At first glance, it's hard to imagine two men less alike.... But one big thing Bush and Churchill may share...Churchill never knew self-doubt. It seems to rarely stalk Bush."[4]

The White House was particularly pleased with the Churchill comparisons. Chief of Staff Andy Card brought a group of reporters into the Oval Office to tell them about Bush's fascination with Churchill and the president's hope to emulate "Churchill's resolve, his humor...his ability to lift a people during a very challenging time." Pointing to a bust of Churchill and a portrait of Lincoln, Card attested to how much Bush treasured them, "It was kind of spontaneous on the president's part to pick out those things."[5]

A *U.S. News & World Report* article repeated Card's claims and elaborated on the Churchill comparison: "Behind the scenes, Bush's advisers describe a man with a new sense of purpose. His latest hero is not drawn from the traditional list of George Washington, Abraham Lincoln, or Franklin Roosevelt. Instead, Bush has become more enthralled than ever with Winston Churchill. Bush finds parallels between his own circumstances and those of the British prime minister who led his country against the Nazi blitz a half-century ago and, with America's help, to ultimate triumph over the Third Reich. Almost since America's terrorist crisis began on September 11th, Bush has told friends how he hopes to emulate Churchill's 'resolve, his humor...his ability to lift a people during a very challenging time,' says White House Chief of Staff Andy Card." The White House staff couldn't directly compare Bush to Lincoln and Churchill, but they could place the suggestion before friendly journalists and count on them to connect the dots, which of course they did.

Connecting Bush to Churchill was part of a White House plan to transform Bush in the public's eye, and according to *U.S. News,* "There is a larger point. Bush's identification with Churchill suggests that he also sees the current crisis as a life-or-death struggle. Aides say he is more methodical and disciplined than ever. He gets to the Oval Office at daybreak, carefully reads his briefing books, and asks plenty of pointed questions, which was not his habit when his presidency started in January. Using the Oval Office as a command center and with Rice at his side, he spends several hours each day doggedly calling foreign leaders to organize the international coalition."[6]

Suddenly Bush was no longer the lazy joker of the past; he was now "methodical and disciplined." The journalists who repackaged Bush into the second coming of Lincoln and Churchill were not just victims of the Administration's spin, they were also satisfying their readers' and viewers' need to believe that George Bush was up to the challenge. Prior to 9/11, even Bush supporters held some doubts about his work habits. Now that the nation was in crisis, people wanted to believe he was the right man for the job. The media echo chamber produced the storyline consumers wanted.

"His Hair is Grayer"

The echo chamber abruptly rang with stories about how Bush suddenly grew up. *Newsweek* claimed "[Bush is] exceeding expectations, learning on the run before our eyes." *Newsday* stated, "We are watching Bush grow into his job." *Time* asserted, "The president is growing before our eyes—not morphing into some completely new kind of leader but evolving in fits and starts and in real time.... The change in the man and his policies is too stark to deny."[7]

As proof of Bush's new maturity, the echo chamber claimed Bush suddenly looked older. *USA Today* wrote, "The furrows in his forehead seem deeper now, and some aides say they think his hair is grayer." The *New York Times* quoted former South Dakota governor William J. Janklow, "Look at his hair. Look at the lines on his face. It's incredible, the toll." MSNBC news anchor Brian Williams declared, "In person, [Bush] has indisputably aged in the job." *Newsweek* concurred, "His Brillo-like hair is graying; there are new, vertical lines on his face that didn't exist a year ago." The *Times* remarked that "Bush seem[s] grayer, graver, and more comfortable in the role" of leader.[8]

The new Bush was not only grayer, he was "more focused." The *Christian Science Monitor* described Bush as "focused in a manner that he wasn't before," and the *Los Angeles Times* claimed Bush devoted himself to the crisis with "single-minded focus." Appearing on *Washington Week in Review, New York Times* reporter Michael Duffy described Bush as "uncluttered in his vision [and] totally focused on this job." NBC correspondent David Gregory harped on the focus theme: "Bush finally found a crisis to focus the sort of discipline that he brought…to the campaign…. He's got a kind of singular focus now…. He just seems so focused…because the Administration…is focused in one area."[9]

The echo chamber also praised Bush's physical fitness. *Fortune:* "[Bush] exercises daily after falling out of the habit and eats healthier food, knowing he must keep up his energy." *Time:* "Bush is sticking to his exercise regimen, watching his diet, and making sure that he gets a decent night's sleep." *U.S. News & World Report:* "Bush's personal regimen suggests a new seriousness." *Newsweek:* "another source of [his] strength is physical conditioning. For Bush it's a concern bordering on obsession, and it's paid off in self-confidence." The *New York Times* quoted Mark McKinnon, Bush's former media consultant: "The fact that he's running a seven-minute mile now attests to the discipline he's bringing to his whole life…. He has more snap, more energy, more focus." A year and a half later, *USA Today* noted approvingly how Bush "gave up sweets just before the [Iraq] War began," as if eating less sugar made him a more capable Commander in Chief.[10] Obviously physical fitness does not necessarily generate mental acuity, but in the days after 9/11, the media was desperate for any evidence to support their storyline that Bush was more focused on his job.

Along with becoming grayer and fitter, Bush apparently acquired greater eloquence. *Fortune:* "His public remarks formerly rare and often fractured are more frequent and self-assured." *Newsweek* claimed Bush is "eloquent in public" and *U.S. News & World Report* described Bush as "speaking with uncharacteristic eloquence and self-reflection." The *Los Angeles Times:* "Bush has spoken...sometimes even eloquently." None of these reports identified specific instances of this eloquence, but it didn't matter. The echo chamber maintained their storyline even when the facts didn't support it. *Time:* "If [Bush] occasionally made side trips through syntax he also showed a level of introspection and analysis that surprised even his aides."[11]

On the rare occasions when the media noted Bush's misstatements they were either downplayed or actually praised. When Bush referred to a "crusade" against Al Qaeda and called Pakistanis "Pakis," the media dismissed these gaffes as unfortunate but insignificant. Some in the media even celebrated Bush's mistakes as reflective of his down-home plainspoken style. *Fortune* wrote, "Even his off-the-cuff remarks have a genuineness that somehow works." According to *Time,* during a speech at the CIA, "Bush said three times that 'the terrorists had misunderestimated America and its leader.' He was right." *Time* went on, "Bush is what the nation needs in a Commander in Chief—simple in his speech, clear in his vision, confident in his ultimate success." The *Los Angeles Times:* "Bush has shown an almost Trumanesque capacity to express what ordinary Americans are thinking." Even liberal pundit Margaret Carlson of *Time* praised Bush for "a singular expressiveness the rest of us lack: Bush's gift of pre-verbal authenticity comes at a time when the most articulate among us have been rendered speechless."[12]

A *New York Times* editorial one month after the terror attacks reaffirmed all the media hype about the new George Bush, "The George W. Bush who addressed the nation...appeared to be a different man from the one who was just barely elected president last year, or even the man who led the country a month ago...more confident, determined...sure of his purpose...in full command of the complex array of political and military challenges...reassuring performance...comfort to an uneasy nation...an assured appearance that should give citizens a sense that their president has done much to master the complexities of this new global crisis."[13]

How did a newspaper that was extremely critical of George Bush since his run for the president suddenly become so laudatory? The answer may be found in a look at Dan Rather's similar conversion to Bushism.

Dan Rather

Like the *New York Times* editorial board, CBS News anchor Dan Rather opposed Bush's presidential run and was skeptical toward the Administration from the very beginning. But several days after 9/11, Rather appeared on the *Late Show with David Letterman* to proclaim, "George Bush is the president. He makes the decisions, and you know, it's just one American. Wherever he wants me to line up, just tell me where, and he'll make the call." Rather later recalled that like most Americans, in and out of the media, he was swept up by patriotic fervor after 9/11: "I don't think you can be too patriotic; when in doubt, I would much prefer to err on the side of too much patriotism as opposed to too little." Upon further reflection and self-examination, Rather observed that his revived patriotism distorted his reporting. "What we are talking about here...is a form of self-censorship. It starts with a feeling of patriotism within oneself. It carries through with a certain knowledge that the country as a whole—and for all the right reasons—felt and continues to feel this surge of patriotism within themselves, and one finds oneself saying, 'I know the right question, but you know what? This is not exactly the right time to ask it.'"[14] Even liberals in the echo chamber could not escape self-censorship after 9/11.

Bill Maher: Public Enemy #1

While Bush found new admirers in the media, his detractors soon learned to shut up. ABC's liberal *Politically Incorrect* host Bill Maher suggested that the hijackers who killed themselves in order to slaughter Americans were not cowards in comparison with the American military, which kills its enemies by launching cruise missiles from thousands of miles away. White House Press Secretary Ari Fleisher denounced Maher and issued a dark warning to other dissenting voices in the media, "People need to watch what they say, watch what they do." ABC quickly cancelled Maher's show. The media fell into a "U.S.A. Number 1" mantra, and anyone who deviated from the storyline didn't get on national television or stay there for long.

Self-censorship

Along with Bill Maher, Osama bin Laden also got bumped from the nation's airwaves. In October 2001, National Security Adviser Condoleezza Rice asked the heads of America's televisions news stations not to show any videos of bin Laden's speeches. The reason she offered was that bin Laden might lace his speeches with coded messages for secret Al Qaeda cells. The fact that secret Al Qaeda cells could still catch bin Laden's speeches on Al Jazeera or on the Internet didn't seem to bother the media executives who voluntarily embraced Rice's ban. Obviously the real reason for the ban was to keep Americans from viewing the videos. If the Administration couldn't kill Osama, at least they could take him off the air. If Americans didn't see him on TV, it would be as if he were dead, and they could begin focusing on another bad guy. The Bush people wanted to control our visual diet and the media executives knuckled under. So much for an independent media.

Commercial pressures also factored into the media's self-censorship. During the Afghanistan War, the chief copy editor of the *Panama City News Herald,* a Florida newspaper, sent out a revealing memo to his staff, "DO NOT USE photos on Page 1A showing civilian casualties from the U.S. war on Afghanistan. Our sister paper in Fort Walton Beach has done so and received hundreds and hundreds of threatening e-mails and the like.... DO NOT USE wire stories that lead with civilian casualties from the U.S. War on Afghanistan. They should be mentioned further down in the story. If the story needs rewriting to play down the civilian casualties, DO IT. The only exception is if the U.S. hits an orphanage, school, or similar facility and kills scores or hundreds of children."[15]

This memo reflects a perception common among news editors and producers after 9/11 that they had to vigilantly filter any news that might be perceived as friendly to the enemy or critical of the U.S. and its president. Greg Mitchell of *Editor and Publisher* told Bill Moyers about the impact of complaints received by newspapers after publishing photos of dead Iraqi soldiers, "Even showing the casualties on the other side is an anti-war statement." Television news organizations like CNN had to be wary during the run up to the Iraq War because the Republican-controlled Congress was debating changes in FCC ownership regulations that would be worth hundreds of millions of dollars.[16] CNN's Christiane Amanpour complained about her network's surrender to political and financial pressure, "The press self-muzzled.... My station was intimidated by the Administration and its foot soldiers at Fox News. And it did, in fact, put a climate of fear and self-censorship...in terms of the kind of broadcast work we did."

In response to Amanpour, Fox News spokesperson Irena Briganti offered a fair and balanced retort,

"Given the choice, it's better to be viewed as a foot soldier for Bush than a spokeswoman for Al Qaeda."[17]

Flag Pins

As if to symbolize how the media jumped on the patriotic bandwagon, TV journalists and talking-heads began adorning their lapels with America's latest fashion craze: flag pins. The late great Peter Jennings, much to his credit, refused to allow flag pins on ABC news broadcasts, but he was alone in his commitment to objectivity. In imitation of Fox News' billowing flag in the corner of the TV screen, NBC altered its peacock logo to include Stars and Stripes and affixed it to all of its TV shows including the sitcoms.

Connecting the Dots

The pseudo-patriotism of the media was more than craven; it bordered on treasonous. Focused on flag-waving and genuflecting, the media ignored the real story of 9/11: how our government failed to protect us from the attack. This failure was obvious from the beginning. Nineteen Middle Eastern guys with shivs thwarted not only airport security but also our multi-billion-dollar intelligence agencies. Yet the mainstream media dropped the story in the months after 9/11 and regurgitated the government's claim that "no one could have possibly connected the dots."

We now know our intelligence agencies could have at least hampered the attack. As early as 1998, the CIA told the FBI that Arab terrorists were plotting to fly a plane packed with explosives into the World Trade Center. The CIA later tracked two members of Al Qaeda (who later became 9/11 hijackers) into the United States, but the CIA refused to pass that information to the FBI because of a bureaucratic turf war. That failure is particularly shameful because the CIA knew Al Qaeda was up to something in the summer of 2001.

In August, the CIA warned British and French officials of "subjects involved in suspicious 747 flight training" and described Al Qaeda member Zacarias Moussaoui, then in FBI custody, as a possible "suicide hijacker." CIA Director George J. Tenet was given a briefing about the Moussaoui case titled "Islamic Extremist Learns to Fly." In the weeks leading up to 9/11, CIA agents reported that in Afghanistan "everyone is talking about an impending attack." Why didn't the CIA tell the FBI about the arrival of Al Qaeda members in the United States especially with all the buzz about an impending attack? They didn't want to surrender their investigation to their bureaucratic rivals in the FBI. If the FBI questioned or conducted surveillance on the two Al Qaeda operatives, they may have uncovered the plot. At the very least, they could have followed those guys to the airport on the morning of 9/11 and prevented them from getting on their flight.

Of course, there's no guarantee that the FBI would have done much with this big tip. The week before the terrorist attacks, a Minneapolis FBI agent told the FAA that Moussaoui was "an Islamic extremist preparing for some future act in furtherance of radical fundamentalist goals" related to flight training. This Minnesota agent wanted to search Moussaoui's computer but was denied permission for reasons that are still unclear. FBI agents in Phoenix were simultaneously reporting to headquarters that an unusual number of Middle Eastern men were enrolled in flight schools and speculated that Al Qaeda might deploy them in a terrorism attack. The FBI field agents requested permission to investigate the sudden popularity of flight school among Arab men, but Washington refused.

The Real 9/11 Cover-up

Was it too much to expect our intelligence agencies to take steps to investigate connections between Al

Qaeda and flying? Was it too taxing for the FBI to issue a warning to airport security to be extra vigilant so that nineteen men with foreign passports and knives couldn't breeze through security? The media echo chamber repeated the phony excuse that laws governing the CIA and FBI prevented more coordination. But even if we're to believe that all these spies and agents have an extremely fastidious respect for the law, it stretches the imagination to think that their directors couldn't figure out a way to inform the FAA that something was up.

Most of the media swallowed the claims that the CIA and FBI failed to register the warning signs because they were unable to "connect the dots" or break some laws. In reality, America's intelligence services couldn't break through the bureaucratic logjam that still continues to hamper our dysfunctional intelligence agencies. If our spies can't figure out how to overcome their bureaucracies in order to protect American lives, we need new spies.

Of course the FBI and CIA aren't going to investigate and expose their own dysfunction. In order to clean up our multi-billion dollar intelligence morass, massive public pressure would have to be placed on our elected officials. But instead of examining the disturbing incompetence of our intelligence agencies, the media echoed their excuses and exonerated them.

If the media conducted an aggressive investigation of our intelligence failures leading up to 9/11, we could have gotten rid of incompetents like CIA director George Tenet who later assured Bush that claims of Iraqi WMDs were a "slam dunk." In the end, the only person to get fired over 9/11 was Bill Maher, and he's good at his job.

One of the reasons so many Americans think 9/11 was an inside job is because they find it hard to believe that we could spend hundreds of billions of dollars on agencies that are so incompetent. Had the media spent time pursuing and airing this story, there might have been a public outcry to fix the bureaucratic mess at the FBI and CIA. Perhaps we also could have shaken up the CIA so that we could have gotten accurate intelligence about Iraq's lack of WMDs in 2002. Thousands of American and Iraqi lives might have been saved if the media had aggressively investigated intelligence failures leading up to 9/11.

There was indeed a 9/11 cover-up. It didn't involve a vast governmental conspiracy to orchestrate a phony terrorist attack. It involved a bunch of high ranking federal bureaucrats covering their mistakes and a media that refused to pursue the story.

No One Could Have Imagined 9/11

Even though the public was kept in the dark about the CIA's and FBI's failures, surely Bush knew that his subordinates blew it. Why didn't he hold any of them accountable? Bush was happy the media was going along with the storyline that no one could have imagined hijackers crashing airplanes into buildings.

On March 24, 2002, CNN noted Secretary of Defense Donald Rumsfeld's claim, "I knew of no intelligence during the six-plus months leading up to September 11th to indicate terrorists would hijack commercial airlines, use them as missiles to fly into the Pentagon or the World Trade Center towers."

USA Today reported a similar remark by President Bush on April 18th, "Nobody in our government, at least, and I don't think the prior government could envision flying airplanes into buildings on such a massive scale."

In May 2002, National Security Adviser Condoleezza Rice said, "I don't think anyone could have predicted that these people would take an airplane and slam it into the World Trade Center."

White House Spokesman Ari Fleischer echoed Rice's remarks, "Never did we imagine what would take place on September 11th where people use those airplanes as missiles and weapons." Initially the press took all these claims at face value, but not everyone was convinced.

The 9/11 Commission

Unlike the media, a group of 9/11 family members refused to buy the government's answers to the key questions about the attack: Why? "They hate us because we're free." And how? "No one could have connected the dots." Bush initially rejected the families' demand that he create an independent investigation into the government's failures to stop the attack. Bush feared that an independent 9/11 commission would expose the skeletons in his own closet. But bowing to pressure in April 2002, Bush proposed that the Republican-controlled Congress conduct the investigation ostensibly because Congress routinely deals with secret information and would not reveal sources and intelligence methods. That didn't satisfy the 9/11 families who finally pushed Bush to create an independent commission headed by former Secretary of State Henry Kissinger.

Kissinger had a long past of orchestrating cover-ups involving his own secret activities including the overthrow of Chile's democratically-elected government under Allende and the covert bombing of Cambodia. He also maintained on-going business relationships with members of the bin Laden family in Saudi Arabia. Bush could be confident that the man who made a career out of "plausible deniability" would not allow anything embarrassing to emerge. The press for the most part praised Kissinger's appointment. Even the *New York Times* noted with approval: "The reaction to the appointment on Capitol Hill and among family members of the September 11th victims was generally positive." But the 9/11 families were actually not as pleased with Kissinger as the *New York Times* claimed and demanded his resignation. Bush eventually agreed to replace Kissinger with former New Jersey Governor Tom Kean.

The media which sat on the sidelines throughout Bush's stonewalling of the 9/11 families also looked the other way when Bush blatantly tried to limit the investigation by blocking the release of information to the Commission members and allocating one of the smallest amounts of funding that any independent commission in recent history has ever received (three million dollars).

After extensive negotiations, Bush and Vice President Cheney agreed to testify before the Commission but under suspicious conditions: 1). They would testify jointly without taking an oath to tell the truth, and 2). Their testimony would not be recorded, and the only record would be the notes taken by one of the Commission staffers, which would not be made public.

The first rule of any investigation is to separate all suspects, so it's harder for them to keep their stories straight. Bush's pre-conditions for testifying should have provoked a major outcry from the major news outlets. But once again, the media refused to raise any questions that would deviate from their Bush-friendly storyline.

9/11 Commission and the Media

One of the 9/11 Commission's key findings ran contrary to the Administration's repeated claims that a 9/11-style attack was unimaginable. According to the Commission, such an attack was "imaginable, and imagined" by the government prior to 9/11. In August 1999, the Federal Aviation Administration issued a report warning of a potential "suicide hijacking operation," and the North American Aerospace Defense Command even "developed exercises to counter such a threat." The Commission reported that on August 6, 2001, Bush was given a Presidential Daily Briefing titled "bin Laden Determined to Strike in U.S." The briefing clearly stated that although the FBI had "not been able to corroborate" a 1998 report that Osama bin Laden was seeking to "hijack a U.S. aircraft.... FBI information since that time indicate[d] patterns of suspicious activity in this country consistent with preparations for hijackings or other types of attacks, including recent surveillance of federal buildings in New York." The claim that no one could have imagined 9/11 was finally discredited.

One might expect that these revelations would cause a media firestorm. But by the time the report was released in 2004, 9/11 was old news and few media organizations chose to reopen the story.

Media Matters, an online media watchdog, performed an interesting experiment. Two months after the release of the 9/11 Commission report on July 20, 2004, they conducted a LexisNexis database search of the "All News" directory to see how many articles reported the inconsistencies between the Bush Administration's claims that no one had imagined a terrorist attack involving airplanes and the 9/11 Commission report. The keyword search results are disturbing: "Rice and predict and airplane and slam and world trade center" came up with six relevant results; "Fleischer and imagine and airplanes as missiles" came up with zero relevant results; "Rice and I could not have imagined" came up with zero relevant results; "Bush and envision flying airplanes into buildings" came up with zero relevant results; and "9/11 Commission and imaginable and imagined" came up with zero relevant results.

The 9/11 report should have sparked a media frenzy. Clearly it contradicted White House claims that no one anticipated a 9/11-style attack. Why wasn't the media interested in this widespread cover-up?

By the summer of 2004, the most influential journalists had moved on to more immediate storylines like the souring war in Iraq and the contentious presidential election. Also the media owned the original storyline that "no one could have imagined 9/11." The fact that the 9/11 report contradicted the original storyline meant that the media would have to revise their initial reporting and admit that they blew the biggest story since Pearl Harbor.

9/11 and the 2004 Election

Pursuing the story about the Administration's false statements about 9/11 would have meant calling into question Bush's honesty in the middle of an election campaign. A media storm on this story may have turned the tide in favor of John Kerry, but the mainstream media prides itself in its supposed non-partisanship. To open this line of questioning less than five months before Americans went to the polls would generate accusations of playing politics. Many Americans would have read a sustained reporting of three-year-old Bush Administration lies as a partisan hit job.

Rather than pursue questions about Bush's veracity about 9/11, the press was feeding off lies about John Kerry not deserving the medals he'd won as a captain of a swift boat in Vietnam. In an attempt to appear "fair and balanced," the national press bent over backwards and lost their balance.

Most importantly, if the media seriously examined the contradictions between what White House officials said about 9/11 and the Commission report, they would have had to question the veracity of the same officials who got us into the Iraq War. After two years of going along with the Administration's lies and spin about Iraq, the media would have had to examine their own failures. And there were plenty.

CHAPTER TWO

WAR DRUMS POUNDING IN THE ECHO CHAMBER

"We are all neo-cons now."
MSNBC's Chris Matthews, April 2003

Selling the War on Iraq

Had the media done its job in the year after 9/11 and exposed the American intelligence community's failures leading up to the attacks, along with the Bush Administration's lies, the public might have been more skeptical toward the neo-con case for war on Iraq. In the lead up to the Iraq War, the media once again echoed the Administration's storyline, and the American public embraced a war that was unnecessary and disastrous.

Now that the Iraq War has killed 4,000 Americans and 150,000 Iraqis, there have been many fine books critiquing the media for allowing Bush to sell the war. Most noteworthy is Frank Rich's *The Greatest Story*

Ever Sold, aptly subtitled *The Decline and Fall of Truth in Bush's America.* These books blame the obvious culprits: George Bush, Dick Cheney, and Karl Rove. However, there are other important culprits in the media echo chamber and government who are also guilty of leading America into the Iraq fiasco.

Bill Clinton's War

Bill Clinton is responsible for more Iraqi deaths than George Bush. During his administration, Clinton maintained a murderous sanctions policy on Iraq that resulted in the deaths of at least half a million Iraqi children. He also started bombing Iraq shortly after taking office in 1993 and never stopped. Throughout his two terms, Clinton enforced the no-fly zones by pounding Iraq with America's longest sustained bombing campaign since Vietnam. During this period, the media devoted virtually no attention to what was really going on in Iraq. As usual the mainstream media rallied around the Commander in Chief during this international confrontation—no matter how senseless and cruel the policy actually was.

Clinton also set the U.S. on the road to eventually invading Iraq by supporting the Iraq Liberation Act of 1998, which placed into law the policy of "regime change." The act stated, "It should be the policy of the

United States to support efforts to remove the regime headed by Saddam Hussein from power in Iraq and to promote the emergence of a democratic government to replace that regime." The Liberation Act authorized Clinton to assist dissident groups by funding anti-Saddam radio and television broadcasts, training anti-Saddam paramilitary forces, and aiding Saddam's political opponents including the corrupt Ahmed Chalabi. The act also authorized Clinton to call upon the United Nations to establish an international criminal tribunal to indict, prosecute, and imprison Saddam Hussein and other Iraqi officials "who are responsible for crimes against humanity, genocide, and other criminal violations of international law." By officially labeling Saddam a war criminal, Bill Clinton eliminated any opportunity for diplomatic negotiation and compromise. Saddam knew he would still be a criminal no matter what he did according to American and international law. There could be no peaceful coexistence between the United States and Saddam Hussein.

Under the terms of the Iraq Liberation Act, the U.S. became officially committed to ousting Saddam: "It is the sense of the Congress that once the Saddam Hussein regime is removed from power in Iraq, the United States should support Iraq's transition to democracy." The House passed the act, 360 to 38; the Senate approved it unanimously. In 2002, George W. Bush repeatedly mentioned this Clinton-backed act as justification for his plans to invade Iraq.

Back in 1991 when George H. W. Bush called an end to the first Gulf War, he and his Secretary of Defense Dick Cheney explained that removing Saddam would necessitate a long military occupation and unleash uncontrollable forces that would destabilize the region. Seven years later, Bill Clinton committed the U.S. to ousting Saddam. The news media coverage of this momentous change was light and whatever discussion arose was overwhelmingly favorable. Why so little debate? In the fall of 1998, the media and the public were much more interested in Bill Clinton's Oval Office fling with Monica Lewinsky.

Wag the Dog

The day before Congress voted to impeach Bill Clinton over the Lewinsky scandal in December 1998, Clinton launched Operation Desert Fox, a four-day bombing campaign on Iraqi targets. Immediately there were suggestions that Clinton was engaging in a "Wag the Dog" media stunt to distract the public from his sex scandal. The echo chamber dismissed this possibility and parroted Clinton's justification for the bombing operation—punishment for Saddam's interference with the U.N.'s weapons inspection. The reality, however, was a lot more complicated that what the media chose to report. Throughout the 1990s, U.N. inspectors had successfully tracked down whatever weapons remained after Saddam destroyed most of his stockpiles in compliance with U.N. mandates. Saddam would have continued to allow the U.N. inspectors to perform their investigations had Bill Clinton not infiltrated the U.N. inspection teams with CIA agents. Saddam Hussein, along with much of the international community, was aware of this CIA operation and understandably refused to tolerate covert U.S. intelligence operations in his country. By authorizing the CIA infiltration, Clinton sabotaged the inspections and then lied to the public about why the Iraqi dictator refused to allow the U.N. inspections to proceed.

Former chief U.N. arms inspector Scott Ritter claimed in his book, *War on Iraq,* "Inspectors were sent in to carry out sensitive inspections that had nothing to do with disarmament but had everything to do with provoking the Iraqis."[1] Why might Clinton want to provoke Saddam?

Surely Bill Clinton knew a military confrontation with Iraq would provide the media with a distraction from the Monica Lewinsky scandal. He also understood that the American public would reflexively rally around him just at the moment when the Republican Congress was set to impeach him.

Clinton's Cowardly War

Over Bill Clinton's final three years in office, the U.S. and Great Britain dropped 1.3 million pounds of bombs in response to violations of the no-fly zones and anti-aircraft fire. In a January 1999 attack, twenty-five missiles hammered Iraq and killed an unknown number of civilians. Clinton said the attack was in response to four Iraqi planes violating the no-fly zones. Coalition forces bombed Iraq on more than 100 days in 1999, sometimes making several bombing runs per day. In the first three months of 1999, U.S.-led forces hit Iraq with 241,000 pounds of bombs—just shy of the 253,000 pounds George Bush dropped in the eight months leading up to the final U.N. resolution authorizing his war on Iraq.

Clinton's war on Iraq was cowardly, not because it was done with cruise missiles and other weapons designed to avoid American casualties (the military should always employ technology to limit casualties); Clinton's war on Iraq was cowardly because the media spared the American public from having to grapple with the horror their leaders inflicted on innocent people. When the television media did cover the story, they simply ran video of the cruise missiles being shot from ships thousands of miles out to sea or jets lifting off from bases in Kuwait. The media filtered images of blown up Iraqis and let the American public off the hook of grappling with the consequences of these bombing operations. Americans also did not see the effects of the sanctions on the sick in Iraqi hospitals that had no medicines. Had the media conducted a genuine exploration of Clinton's policies, the public would have had to look war in the face and accept responsibility for its brutal consequences. The echo chamber's silence on the morality of Clinton's Iraq War insulated Americans from reality and kept them oblivious like a bunch of children.

By the time Bush began his own marketing campaign for an invasion of Iraq, a compliant, lazy media and an ignorant public had already signed on to war with Iraq—a war that Americans had been tacitly supporting without discourse, debate, or dissent since the Clinton administration. Even before the Bush Administration began to sell the war, a September 2001 *Washington Post* poll found thirty-nine percent of respondents thought overthrowing Saddam must be done "even if he is not linked to the 9/11 attacks," and that was before the Bush PR machine kicked into gear.

Fast forward to the 2008 presidential election campaign where Bill Clinton tries to counter Barack Obama's opposition to Bush's invasion of Iraq by claiming he also opposed it back in 2003. Not only is this false (Clinton vocally and enthusiastically supported Bush's war), but Clinton *started* the war on Saddam Hussein. George Bush just escalated the war with an outright invasion.

William Kristol: Neo-con Artist

In the brain-dead world of American mainstream media, William Kristol is considered an intellectual. If he had been the son of "Joe Pickup Truck" instead of Irving Kristol, he would be just another neo-con whacko. The media began fawning over William Kristol in the 1980s when he was writing speeches for that intellectual giant Dan Quayle. He penned Quayle's absurd denunciation of TV's single-mom Murphy Brown as a symptom of the permissive society. Kristol seems to specialize in hyping fictitious bogeymen whether they are unwed sitcom characters or paper tiger dictators like Saddam Hussein.

In 1997, Kristol leveraged his reputation as a big thinker to form a conservative think tank called the Project for a New American Century (PNAC). His idea was to bring together "great minds" like Dick Cheney,

Donald Rumsfeld, and Paul Wolfowitz to concoct plans for a new world order in which the United States would use its vast technological and financial advantage over the rest of the world to secure control over the planet's natural resources—meaning oil.

In September 2000, the PNAC issued a blueprint for a Pax Americana called "Rebuilding America's Defenses: Strategies, Forces, and Resources for a New Century." The report called for unprecedented hikes in military spending, a proliferation of military bases in Central Asia and the Middle East, toppling of resistant governments, scraping international treaties, controlling the world's energy sources, militarization of outer space, dominance over cyberspace, and the possible use of nuclear weapons on anyone who opposed American hegemony. Quite a tall order, unless....

The PNAC report conceded that its plan for world domination would take decades "absent some catastrophic and catalyzing event—like a new Pearl Harbor." On September 11, 2001, Kristol and the neo-cons got their wish.

9/11: The New Pearl Harbor

A day after 9/11, PNAC members Secretary of Defense Don Rumsfeld and his undersecretary Paul Wolfowitz began planning military operations against

Iraq. Richard Clarke, head of counter terrorism under Clinton and Bush, was baffled by all the talk about Iraq during meetings on 9/11. Clarke knew Al Qaeda had nothing to do with Iraq. But Don Rumsfeld saw 9/11 as an opportunity to fulfill PNAC plans. When Pentagon intelligence agents reported back to him that there were no ties between Al Qaeda and Saddam Hussein, Rumsfeld sent them back to look again.

When the Administration launched its campaign for war on Iraq in the fall of 2002, the media hailed Kristol as "the intellectual architect" of Bush's policy of using the military to spread democracy in the Middle East. Kristol went on the talk show circuit pushing the same rumors and faulty intelligence that the Administration was simultaneously peddling.

He was also always ready to offer reassuring predictions of war's impending success: "[The war in Iraq] could have terrifically good effects throughout the Middle East" (September 18, 2002). Removing Saddam "would start a chain reaction in the Arab world that would be very healthy" (November 21, 2002). "Very few wars in American history were prepared better or more thoroughly than this one by this president" (March 1, 2003). "I think we'll be vindicated when we discover the weapons of mass destruction and when we liberate the people of Iraq"

(March 5, 2003). "There has been a certain amount of pop sociology...that the Shiia can't get along with the Sunni...there's almost no evidence of that at all" (April 4, 2003). "The first two battles of this new era are now over. The battles of Afghanistan and Iraq have been won decisively and honorably" (April 28, 2003). Debates over an Iraqi constitution reveal "the willingness on the part of the diverse ethnic and religious groups to disagree—peacefully and then to compromise" (March 22, 2004). "It is much more likely that the situation in Iraq will stay more or less the same or improved in either case. Republicans will benefit from being the party of victory" (November 30, 2005).

Kristol was obviously a zealot and a neo-con ideologue, but the media treated him like a profound thinker and a journalist who possessed a well-informed, nuanced view of the world. Nothing could be further from the truth.

Even before the war turned into a disaster and all of Kristol's optimistic predictions turned out to be wrong, anyone who actually understood the complexities of the Middle East knew that he was delusional. A Western military occupation of Iraq was inevitably going to breed terrorism and chaos, not democracy and regional harmony. Today, after five years of bloodshed in Iraq, one might expect Kristol would finally be dismissed as a charlatan. But in December 2007, the *New York Times* welcomed Kristol to its prestigious slate of regular columnists—another example of someone "failing his way to the top."

Branding the "War on Terror"

In order for the Bush Administration to channel the anger over 9/11 toward Saddam Hussein, they tried to find evidence of an alliance between Al Qaeda and Saddam. Rumsfeld gave his Undersecretary Douglas Feith responsibility for heading two Pentagon groups charged with drawing up talking points outlining the rumored ties between Saddam and Al Qaeda. Colin Powell received these crackpot memos and started privately referring to Feith's operation as the Gestapo.[2]

Even without any evidence of such collaboration, the Administration could fudge things rhetorically. That's why they came up with the brand name "War on Terror." Saddam Hussein and many others could be guilty of terror even if they weren't terrorists. Ultimately the Administration didn't need credible evidence of Saddam/Al Qaeda alliance. They just needed a credulous media and an echo chamber that repeated the brand "War on Terror" and splashed it across American TV screens every night.

Marketing the War

The White House understood how vulnerable the media was to manipulation. When they decided to invade Iraq in the summer of 2002, a task force was formed called White House Iraq Group, or WHIG, to "educate the public" about Saddam's threat. A senior official who participated in WHIG called it "an internal working group, like many formed for priority issues, to make sure each part of the White House was fulfilling its responsibilities." "Responsibilities" meant selling the Iraq War.

Meeting weekly in the Situation Room, WHIG's regular participants were either communications specialists like Karl Rove, Karen Hughes, Mary Matalin, and Scooter Libby or national security experts like Condoleezza Rice and her deputy Stephen J. Hadley.[3] This group's work blurred the lines between marketing strategy and national security and between slogan and fact. Like any marketing campaign, every speech and talking point that came out of WHIG massaged the facts to sell the product. In this case the product was war.

Chief of Staff Andrew Card acknowledged this PR campaign in an interview with the *New York Times* in September 2002. Card explained that although the Administration had a good case against Saddam that summer, it would have to wait until the fall because "from a marketing point of view, you don't introduce new products in August." The anniversary of 9/11 that September provided a great moment for this product launch.

"Beat the Press" with Tim Russert

No member of the media bears greater responsibility for helping the Administration sell the Saddam/Al Qaeda connection than Tim Russert. Russert, the host of the longest running, highest-rated political talk show, acquired the reputation for being a hard-nosed interrogator of his guests. His supposed tenacity and jowly countenance led many in the echo chamber to call him a "bulldog,"[4] but an analysis of his spots with Dick Cheney during the lead-up to Iraq reveals Russert to be more lap dog than bulldog.

When Cheney appeared on *Meet the Press* five days after 9/11, Russert started the discussion of an Al Qaeda/Saddam connection: "Saddam Hussein, your old friend, his government had this to say, 'The American cowboy is rearing the fruits of crime against humanity.' If we determine that Saddam Hussein is also harboring terrorists, and there's a track record there, would we have any reluctance of going after Saddam Hussein?"

Dick Cheney replied, "No."

Russert then pestered Cheney on the supposed Al Qaeda/Saddam connection, "Do we have evidence that he's harboring terrorists?"

Cheney admitted, "There have been some activities related to terrorism by Saddam Hussein." But he insisted, "At this stage the focus is on Al Qaeda."

Russert kept pressing, "Do we have any evidence linking Saddam Hussein or Iraqis to this operation?"

Cheney responded with an unambiguous "No."

The Administration did not start the public discussion of the Al Qaeda/Saddam connection. The media did. In this case, Tim Russert raised Saddam's possible links to 9/11 even when Dick Cheney unambiguously denied any evidence of such connections.

On the face of it, Russert was simply doing his job. A Saddam Hussein/Al Qaeda connection would have been important news, but there was much more to Russert's solicitous questioning. During the Scooter Libby trial, Cheney's Communications Director testified that when the vice president's office needed to do damage control over Libby's outing of Valerie Plame, "I suggested we put the vice president on *Meet the Press*, which was a tactic we often used. It's our best format."[5]

Meet the Press was Cheney's "best format" because Russert was a hawk on Iraq from the very beginning. Cheney knew that. Two months later, on December 9, 2001, Cheney chose Russert's show to voice for the first time evidence of a Saddam/Al Qaeda connection, "Well, what we now have that's developed since you and I last talked, Tim, of course, was that report that's been pretty well confirmed, that [Muhammad Atta] did go to Prague, and he did meet with a senior official of the Iraqi intelligence service in Czechoslovakia last April, several months before the attack."

Cheney continued, "Now, what the purpose of that was, what transpired between them, we simply don't know at this point. But that's clearly an avenue that we want to pursue."

Russert then asked a "question" that supported Cheney's claims, "What we do know is that Iraq is harboring terrorists...that Abdul Ramini Yazen, who helped bomb the World Trade Center back in 1993, according to Louis Freeh, was hiding in his native Iraq.... If they're harboring terrorists, why not go in and get them?" Russert not only pushed the connection between Saddam and terrorists in the question, he enthusiastically suggested invading Iraq to "go in and get them."

Nine months later on September 8, 2002, days before the first anniversary of the 9/11 attacks, Cheney again went on *Meet the Press* to connect Saddam with terrorism.

Cheney: "But come back to 9/11 again, and one of the real concerns about Saddam Hussein, as well, is his biological weapons capability; the fact that he may, at some point, try to use smallpox, anthrax, plague, some other kind of biological agent against other nations, possibly including even the United States. So this is not just a one-dimensional threat. This just isn't a guy who's now back trying once again to build nuclear weapons. It's the fact that we've also seen him in these other areas, in chemicals, but also especially in biological weapons, increase his capacity to produce and deliver these weapons upon his enemies."

Russert: "But if he ever did that, would we not wipe him off the face of the earth?"

Cheney: "Who did the anthrax attack last fall, Tim? We don't know."

Russert: "Could it have been Saddam?"

Cheney: "I don't know. I don't know who did it. I'm not here today to speculate on or to suggest that he did."

It sounds like speculating about Saddam's 9/11 connections was *precisely* why Cheney was on *Meet the Press* that morning. And Russert was there to excitedly prompt Cheney through all his speculation about Saddam's connection with the anthrax letters. Russert even contributed his own anti-Saddam hyperbole asking about "wip[ing] him off the face of the earth." In the months after 9/11, everyone in the White House was talking tough (Bush, Cheney, Rumsfeld, and even the miscast Ari Fleisher), and the press loved it. Russert seemed to have gotten into the trash-talking, macho act.

In the same interview Russert once again tried to coax Cheney to tie Saddam to 9/11, "Has anything changed [since Cheney's last appearance] in your mind?"

Cheney: "Well, I want to be very careful about how I say this. I'm not here today to make a specific allegation that Iraq was somehow responsible for 9/11. I can't say that. On the other hand, since we did that interview, new information has come to light. And we spent time looking at that relationship between Iraq, on the one hand, and the Al Qaeda organization on the other. And there has been reporting that suggests that there have been a number of contacts over the years. We've seen in connection with the hijackers, of course, Mohamed Atta, who was the lead hijacker, did apparently travel to Prague on a number of occasions. And on at least one occasion, we have reporting that places him in Prague with a senior Iraqi intelligence official a few months before the attack on the World Trade Center. The debates about, you know, was he there or wasn't he there. Again, it's the intelligence business."

The CIA had already dismissed the story of a meeting between Atta and Saddam's intelligence agents in Prague, but Cheney presented it as fact. Cheney managed to both lie and evade the question when Russert asked, "What does the CIA say about that and the president?" Cheney answered, "It's credible. But, you know, I think a way to put it would be it's unconfirmed at this point. We've got—"

Russert then cut Cheney off. He could have asked Cheney to clarify the CIA's assessment of whether Atta met with Iraqi intelligence. But Russert wasn't interested in challenging Cheney or probing into the CIA's doubts. Instead he prompted the vice president for more on the Saddam/Al Qaeda connection, "Anything else?"

Cheney: "There is, again, I want to separate out 9/11 from the other relationships between Iraq and the Al Qaeda organization. But there is a pattern of relationships going back many years. And in terms of exchanges and in terms of people, we've had recently since the operations in Afghanistan—we've seen Al Qaeda members operating physically in Iraq and off the territory of Iraq. We know that Saddam Hussein has, over the years, been one of the top state sponsors of terrorism for nearly twenty years. We've had this recent weird incident where the head of the Abu Nidal organization, one of the world's most noted terrorists, was killed in Baghdad. The announcement was made by the head of Iraqi intelligence. The initial announcement said he'd shot himself. When they dug into that, though, he'd shot himself four times in the head. And speculation has been that, in fact, somehow, the Iraqi government or Saddam Hussein had him eliminated to avoid potential embarrassment by virtue of the fact that he was in Baghdad and operated in Baghdad. So it's a very complex picture to try to sort out. And—"

Russert: "But no direct link?"

Cheney: "I can't. I'll leave it right where it's at. I don't want to go beyond that. I've tried to be cautious and restrained in my comments, and I hope that everybody will recognize that."

Russert then ended the interview allowing Cheney to dance around the question about a direct link between Saddam and Al Qaeda. Cheney was surely relieved. He knew most of his claims came from suspect informants who were already being challenged by American intelligence agencies and foreign governments. Cheney was clearly throwing everything he had against the wall, hoping something would stick. Russert could have challenged Cheney on any of his claims or demanded more specifics, but in the end he passively allowed Cheney to "leave it right where it's at" by pretending that he'd said too much already.

Dick Cheney's Big Lie

Cheney was the master of an old propaganda tactic "The Big Lie," which Adolf Hitler defined in *Mein Kampf* as a lie so "colossal" that no one would believe that someone "could have the impudence to distort the truth so infamously." The trick is to tell a lie big enough and often enough that people assume it must be true, despite the facts.

On October 21, 2002, James Risen of the *New York Times* revealed in early 2002 that Czech president Vaclav Havel quietly revealed to the White House that there was no evidence of a meeting between Atta and Czech intelligence in Prague.[6] Havel did not go public with the information because he did not want to embarrass Administration officials, like Cheney, who were aggressively pushing the story as fact. Not only did Cheney ignore Havel's warning and continue repeating the story of the Prague meeting, but he also continued to deploy it even after the *Times* reported it to be false. Only after the 9/11 Commission officially refuted the story in 2004, did Cheney stop using the story.[7]

Cheney got away with deploying such unsubstantiated rumors and accusations because the press was not doing its job. Like Tim Russert, most of the media bowed down to Cheney, left his falsehoods unchecked, and echoed them. The result was nothing short of mass delusion. Two weeks after 9/11, a CBS News/*New York Times* poll found that just six percent of the American public thought that Saddam collaborated with Al Qaeda.[8] Two years later, after hearing the Big Lie rattle around the echo chamber, sixty-nine percent of the American public believed Saddam helped the 9/11 terrorists.[9] Talk about Mission Accomplished!

Ahmed Chalabi: Dissident for Hire

Iraq's alleged nuclear program was the other Big Lie that convinced a majority of Americans to support the war. On August 26, 2002, Dick Cheney admitted that proving Saddam had chemical or biological weapons might not be enough to scare Americans into launching a preemptive war on Iraq, "I am familiar with the arguments against taking action in the case of Saddam Hussein. Some concede that Saddam is evil, power-hungry, and a menace—but that, until he crosses the threshold of actually possessing nuclear weapons, we should rule out any preemptive action." Cheney was right, most Americans would have tolerated an Iraq with chemical or biological WMDs. But a nuclear bomb was another story.

The Administration's campaign to convince Americans that Saddam had crossed the nuclear threshold depended on a thoroughly corrupt dissident for hire, Ahmed Chalabi. Since the passage of the Iraq Liberation Act, the U.S. government paid Chalabi vast sums to lead a so-called Iraqi resistance group even though he had not lived in Iraq for four decades and was a fugitive from Jordan after being convicted of embezzling $70 million from a bank he founded. Yet the U.S. government gave Chalabi's anti-Saddam group $4.3 million in American taxpayers' money, which he immediately began to embezzle. In the lead up to war, the Pentagon gave Chalabi a whopping $100 million. What did the Pentagon get in exchange? Chalabi fed the White House, State Department, military intelligence, and the press any story that helped sell the case for war.

The embezzler/fugitive was a great salesman. In an appearance on ABC News, Chalabi, who hadn't lived in Iraq since the 1950s, promised that the Iraqi people would greet U.S. troops as liberators and offer little resistance. Cheney and other Administration officials soon began parroting Chalabi's optimistic prediction which rattled around the media echo chamber and became the conventional wisdom.

Chalabi's rosy prediction not only fooled the media, it also tragically blinded the Pentagon to the possibility of a post-Saddam insurgency. Instead of listening to General Eric Shinseki's warning that occupying a country the size of California would require several hundred thousand soldiers, Rumsfeld and Wolfowitz sent an underpowered force that was able to oust Saddam's government but incapable of restoring order.

Military officials now say the Pentagon's extremely optimistic predictions about the stability of post-Saddam contributed to the failure to provide the troops with adequate body armor and vehicles that could withstand IEDs. Even after it was clear that U.S. troops were fighting a widespread insurgency, Rumsfeld reassured a fawning press that resistance came from a small number of Baathist "dead-enders." While troops began hanging their crotch protectors under their arms to protect their sides, Rumsfeld did nothing to address the lack of body armor.

A 2006 Pentagon study found that eighty percent of the Marines killed in Iraq from wounds to the upper body could have survived if they had had extra body armor. More than 300 young Americans might still be alive today if the Pentagon had based its pre-war planning on facts instead of spin.[10]

Judith Miller

Ahmed Chalabi was the main source for *New York Times* reporter Judith Miller, another charlatan responsible for selling America on Saddam's nuclear program. Miller had been working on stories about Saddam's weapons programs since the mid 1990's. She got most of her information from a circle of Iraqi defectors who claimed to have firsthand knowledge of Saddam's activities, but like Chalabi were opportunistic self-promoters who knew nothing.

In December 2001, Chalabi arranged for Miller to meet with Adnan Ihsan Saeed al-Haideri, an Iraqi construction contractor who renovated Saddam's palaces and claimed to know about Saddam's WMD programs. Miller's story, based on this interview, landed on the *Times'* December 20, 2001, front page under the headline "Iraqi Tells of Renovations at Sites for Chemical and Nuclear Arms."

The article stated, "An Iraqi defector who described himself as a civil engineer said he personally worked on renovations of secret facilities for biological, chemical and nuclear weapons in underground wells, private villas and under the Saddam Hussein Hospital in Baghdad as recently as a year ago."[11]

What kind of a weapons program would operate out of an underground well, a private villa, or under a hospital in the middle of a capital city crawling with diplomats and spies? A reasonably skeptical reporter would have dismissed this defector as unreliable within five minutes, but not Judy Miller, who admitted in the article that "there was no means to independently verify Mr. Saeed's allegations." She believed him because "he seemed familiar with key Iraqi officials in the military establishment, with many facilities previously thought to be associated with unconventional weapons, and with Iraq itself." She also cited a character reference from a representative of Chalabi's group who served in the army with Saeed and "had known him for many years and trusted him."[12] Three days *before* Miller's interview with Saeed, the CIA got results from a polygraph test that revealed Saeed was a liar.[13]

Miller's reporting was not just shabby. It was dangerous, and she knew it. "If verified," Miller wrote, "Mr. Saeed's allegations would provide ammunition to officials within the Bush Administration who have been arguing that Mr. Hussein should be driven from power partly because of his unwillingness to stop making weapons of mass destruction." Miller's editors at the *Times* also understood that Saeed's story was both dubious and dangerous but ran it anyway.

The Saeed story revealed a disturbing pattern that Miller often repeated. Chalabi provided the same bogus stories to Miller and Administration hawks. Miller then sought confirmation of the stories from Administration hawks who appeared in her reports as "unnamed senior Administration officials." Administration hawks then went on TV to cite Miller's stories as further reasons why the U.S. had to get rid of Saddam. This is the echo chamber in action.

Aluminum Tubes and Tin Foil Hats

When the Administration began planning to sell the Iraq War in the summer of 2002, Miller teamed up with Michael Gordon to work on investigating Saddam's nukes. Gordon, the paper's chief military correspondent, was a perfect match for Miller. He was an anti-Saddam hawk who published a book titled, *The Generals' War: The Inside Story of the Conflict in the Gulf,* condemning George H.W. Bush's decision to leave Saddam in power back in 1991.

In the summer of 2002, Scooter Libby chose the credulous Miller to leak classified information about a shipment of aluminum tubes that were intercepted on their way to Iraq. Libby probably knew Miller would swallow his claim that the tubes were meant to be used in a nuclear centrifuge. Miller and Gordon took the bait and wrote up a report that appeared on the front page on September 8, 2002: "In the last fourteen months, Iraq has sought to buy thousands of specially designed aluminum tubes, which American officials believe were intended as components of centrifuges to enrich uranium."[14]

A year before Miller's article appeared, a U.S. government report filed by retired Oak Ridge National Laboratory physicist Houston G. Wood III concluded that the tubes were not meant for centrifuges at all. U.S. Department of Energy and the International Atomic Energy Agency confirmed Iraq's claims that the tubes were to be used in conventional artillery rockets. The State Department's Bureau of Intelligence and Research would later confirm that the aluminum tubes were for rockets after U.S.

analysts in Iraq collected and photographed identical tubes marked with the logo of an Italian rocket manufacturer and the words "81mm rocket" in English.[15] In a follow up article on September 13th, Miller and Gordon cited "the intelligence agencies' unanimous view that the type of [aluminum] tubes that Iraq has been seeking are used to make such centrifuges." In reality there was a lot of disagreement within the government about the tubes, which Miller could have discovered with a few phone calls.

However, Miller wasn't interested in dissenting opinions that might take the punch out of her aluminum tube story.[16] She fully embraced neo-con hysterics: "Hard-liners are alarmed that American intelligence underestimated the pace and scale of Iraq's nuclear program before Baghdad's defeat in the Gulf War. Conscious of this lapse in the past, they argue that Washington dare not wait until analysts have found hard evidence that Mr. Hussein has acquired a nuclear weapon." Miller fatefully repeated a line that one of her unnamed officials fed her, "The first sign of a 'smoking gun,' they argue, may be a mushroom cloud."

After the truth about the aluminum tubes came out, Miller was confronted about how she allowed herself to be duped by her Administration sources:

"[M]y job isn't to assess the government's information and be an independent intelligence analyst myself. My job is to tell readers of the *New York Times* what the government thought about Iraq's arsenal."[17]

That's not journalism, that's stenography. The job of the reporter is not to just report leaks from unnamed government officials but to sift through all available information including dissenting voices to get as close to the truth as possible. Anyone who claims to be a "journalist" must uphold this responsibility especially if they work for a prominent publication like the *New York Times*. By failing so miserably at her job, Miller transformed the most influential newspaper in the world into a Bush Administration mouthpiece and helped push the U.S. down the road to a costly and unnecessary war.

Miller and the *Times* understood the stakes. As the aluminum tube/mushroom cloud article explained, "Mr. Hussein's dogged insistence on pursuing his nuclear ambitions, along with what defectors described in interviews as Iraq's push to improve and expand Baghdad's chemical and biological arsenals, have brought Iraq and the United States to the brink of war." Yet the reporter and her editors continued to play right into the neo-con plan to dupe America into a war with Saddam.

Mushroom Clouds and Smoking Guns

It wasn't a coincidence that Miller's piece on the aluminum tubes ran on the Sunday before the first anniversary of 9/11. Nor was it coincidental that Administration officials were scheduled to appear that same Sunday morning on all the political TV talk shows. All the shows were doing 9/11 anniversary coverage which added a sense of urgency to the discussion of Miller's story. On CNN's *Later Edition with Wolf Blitzer,* National Security Adviser Condoleezza Rice repeated one of Miller's lines, "We don't want the smoking gun to be a mushroom cloud." The Administration fed lines to Miller who fed those same lines back to the Administration.

On *Face the Nation,* Bob Schieffer reviewed the events of 9/11 with Don Rumsfeld and then turned to the Miller article.

Bob Schieffer: "Well, let me ask you then. Tell me about the seriousness of the problem. We read in the *New York Times* today a story that says that Saddam Hussein is closer to acquiring nuclear weapons. Does he have nuclear weapons? Is there a smoking gun here?"

Don Rumsfeld: "Smoking gun is an interesting phrase. It implies that what we're doing here is law enforcement, that what we're looking for is a case that we can take into a court of law and prove beyond a reasonable doubt. The problem with that is the way one gains absolutely certainty as to whether a dictator like Saddam Hussein has a nuclear weapon is if he uses it."

Schieffer: "Uh-huh."

Rumsfeld: "—and that's a little late."

Rumsfeld then asked listeners to "imagine a September 11th with weapons of mass destruction," which would kill "tens of thousands of innocent men, women and children."

On *Fox News Sunday,* Secretary of State Colin Powell said, "As we saw in reporting just this morning [in the *Times*], [Saddam] is still trying to acquire, for example, some of the specialized aluminum tubing one needs to develop centrifuges that would give you an enrichment capability."

On *Meet the Press,* Dick Cheney pretended he was surprised by Miller's report. "There's a story in the *New York Times* this morning, this is. I don't, and I want to attribute the *Times*. I don't want to talk about, obviously, specific intelligence sources." Cheney knew his Chief of Staff gave Miller the classified information that formed the basis for the story about the aluminum tubes. He just pretended that she uncovered something herself and then cited her article as proof of his claims about Saddam's nuclear weapons program.

"It's now public that, in fact, he has been seeking to acquire, and we have been able to intercept and prevent him from acquiring through this particular channel, the kinds of tubes that are necessary to build a centrifuge."

Here's another perfect example of the echo chamber. A leak from Dick Cheney's office to Judith Miller became the basis for a front page *Sunday New York Times* article. Administration officials then went on Sunday talk shows to cite the *Times* article about aluminum tubes as independent confirmation of their argument for war. Over the subsequent weeks leading up to the congressional vote on war, everyone in the echo chamber who wanted to argue in favor referred to the aluminum tubes.

Even George Bush cited the tubes as evidence of an Iraqi nuclear program in a September 12, 2002, speech to the U.N. General Assembly, "Iraq has made several attempts to buy high-strength aluminum tubes used to enrich uranium for a nuclear weapon." Bush also evoked Miller's mushroom cloud on October 7th, "Facing clear evidence of peril, we cannot wait for the final proof—the smoking gun—that could come in the form of a mushroom cloud."

In reality, the smoking gun was in the form of an aluminum tube, not a mushroom cloud.

In that October 7th speech, Bush also pushed the Iraq/Al Qaeda connection: "We know that Iraq and Al Qaeda have high-level contacts that go back decades. Some Al Qaeda leaders who fled Afghanistan went to Iraq…. We've learned that Iraq has trained Al Qaeda members in bomb-making and poisons and poisons and deadly gases." Within a week Congress voted overwhelmingly in support of the Administration's war resolution.

Congressional Democrats Trapped in the Echo Chamber

Cowardly Congressional Democrats felt powerless against the echo chamber. They knew that if they opposed the Iraq War resolution, they would be called unpatriotic or naïve in the face of Saddam's alleged nuclear bomb program and his supposed Al Qaeda ties. But what was really naïve was believing that the Administration and the echo chamber were presenting an accurate picture of Saddam's threat. Yet only fourteen Democratic senators even bothered to read the National Intelligence Estimate (NIE) before voting on the war. The NIE was full of caveats about Saddam's WMDs and his ties to Al Qaeda. The facts and intelligence, however, did not matter to Democrats facing a tough midterm election the following month. As Senate Leader Democrat Tom Daschle revealed on *Meet the Press,* his party just wanted to "get this question of Iraq behind us" and hopefully the media would change its focus to the economy or health care before Americans went to the polls in November 2002.

The congressional Democrats' timidity on Iraq contributed to the pro-war tone of the media coverage. Doyle McManus, Washington Bureau Chief of the *Los Angeles Times,* blamed congressional Democrats for his paper's one-sided coverage of the pre-war debate, "We're not in the habit of ginning up debate that's not out there. The debate has been slow to come about— in many ways because the Democratic Party, or at least the Congressional Democratic Party, decided not to hold a debate on this."[18] For McManus and the mainstream press, if Congressional Democrats didn't generate debate about the Iraq War, no debate was newsworthy. Although millions of academics, activists, and ordinary Americans knew the war was a bad idea, they didn't fit the storyline of an America united behind a bipartisan war.

Congressional Democrats and dissenting journalists got caught in a vicious cycle. Democrats wouldn't challenge Bush because they saw no public debate on the war in the media, and the media would not generate stories about the public debate because the congressional Democrats didn't challenge Bush.

The *New York Times* vs. the U.N.

Miller's part in the Iraq saga did not end with her aluminum tube story. After the craven Democrats buckled in the face of the echo chamber and anxious voters, the only way war could be avoided was if the U.N. could prove that there were no WMDs in Iraq. Proving a negative is always difficult, but Miller did her part to make sure it didn't happen by further hyping the Iraqi threat and dismissing the U.N. weapons inspection effort.

In a September 18, 2002, article titled, "Threats and Reponses: Inspection; Verification Is Difficult at Best, Say the Experts, and Maybe Impossible," Miller repeated the Administration's line that the U.N. weapons inspectors were on a fool's mission. "Verifying Iraq's assertions that it has abandoned weapons of mass destruction, or finding evidence that it has not done so, may not be feasible, according to officials and former weapons inspectors."[19] In other words, even if the inspectors don't find WMDs, the United States should go to war anyway.

On December 3, 2002, "C.I.A. Hunts Iraq Tie to Soviet Smallpox," Miller once again based her story on unidentified sources. "The C.I.A. is investigating an informant's accusation that Iraq obtained a particularly virulent strain of smallpox from a Russian scientist who worked in a smallpox lab in Moscow during Soviet times."[20] No basis for the report existed other than a CIA investigation into a rumor spread by an unidentified informant. This should never have made it to the pages of the *Times*. But the opportunity to run a headline combining the words "Iraq" and "Smallpox" was too good for the editors to pass up—pure fear mongering.

On January 24, 2003, Miller impuns the U. N. inspectors' inconclusive findings: "Former Iraqi scientists, military officers and contractors have provided American intelligence agencies with a portrait of Saddam Hussein's secret programs to develop and conceal chemical, biological and nuclear weapons that is starkly at odds with the findings so far of the United Nations weapons inspectors."[21] Miller was doing exactly what Administration spokespeople were doing—dismissing the U.N. inspections as a waste of time so that they could begin bombing and fulfilling their neo-con dreams.

On the first night of the war, Miller appeared on CNN to assure the American public that large numbers of Saddam's WMD factories would soon be over-run by U.S. forces. "One person in Washington told me that the list could total more than 1,400 of these sites."[22] Once again, Miller made a bogus claim based on an unnamed source.

"Hero to the Press"

The *New York Times* eventually apologized for Miller's shameful reporting and encouraged her "retirement" in a pathetic attempt to distance themselves from her irresponsible yarns. (They allowed Gordon to keep his job.) Miller served almost three months in prison for refusing to cooperate with prosecutors and reveal that Scooter Libby leaked Valerie Plame's name to her. For that, the echo chamber hailed Miller as a hero. Chris Matthews couldn't contain himself when she appeared on MSNBC's *Hardball*: "Judy, you're a hero to the press. You are definitely a woman to be trusted with secrets and thank you for coming on this program." All was forgiven in the echo chamber.

Burying Dissent at the Washington Post

The *Washington Post*, the nation's second most respected newspaper, also caught the war fever. From late August through early September 2002, when the White House rolled out its marketing campaign for the war, the *Post* ran several front-page articles with alarming headlines: "Cheney Says Iraqi Strike Is Justified: Hussein Poses Threat, He Declares," Dana Milbank, August 27, 2002; "Bush, Blair Decry Hussein: Iraqi Threat Is Real, They Say," Karen DeYoung, September 8, 2002; and "War Cabinet Argues for Iraq Attack: Bush Advisers Cite U.S. Danger," Mike Allen, September 9, 2002.

Strictly speaking, these articles were not about Iraqi's WMDs. They were about the Administration's claims about WMDs. The *Post* didn't even bother to find independent confirmation. By echoing the Administration's accusations on the front page, the *Post* was essentially confirming them.

In mid-September 2002, *Post* staff writer Joby Warrick submitted an article about a report from the Institute for Science and International Security that cast doubt about the aluminum tubes—the key evidence of Saddam's alleged nuclear program. The *Post* editors buried Warrick's report on A18. Over the subsequent months, the *Post* published several other front-page articles, not about the actual programs but on the Administration's claims about Iraq's nuclear weapons and purported ties to Al Qaeda: "Bush Cites

Urgent Iraqi Threat," Karen DeYoung, October 8, 2002, and "U.S. Suspects Al Qaeda Got Nerve Agent From Iraqis," Barton Gellman, December 12, 2002.

When staff writers Walter Pincus and Dana Priest reported on January 30, 2003, that senior Administration officials considered the White House's evidence against Iraq "still circumstantial," their article appeared on page A14.

In the week prior to the March 20, 2003, invasion of Iraq, the *Post* once again buried an article by Pincus that cited serious doubts among "senior intelligence analysts," placing it on page A17. Pincus and Milbank also submitted an article about how Administration accusations had been "challenged—and in some cases disproved—by the United Nations, European governments and even U.S. intelligence reports." That one appeared on page A13.

Pincus later said his editors had failed to "put things on the front page that would make a difference."[23] As Pincus explained, the placement of these stories was no accident. "The front pages of the *New York Times,* the *Washington Post,* and the *Los Angeles Times* are very important in shaping what other people think. They're like writing a memo to the White House." But the *Post*'s editors, he said, "went through a whole phase in which they didn't put things on the front page that would make a difference." In other words, the *Post* editors buried stories that would have helped avoid an unnecessary war.

Some *Washington Post* reporters lobbied their editors to give greater prominence to stories that questioned the Administration's evidence, but they were rebuffed. "The paper was not front-paging stuff," said Pentagon correspondent Thomas Ricks. "Administration assertions were on the front page. Things that challenged the Administration were on A18 on Sunday or A24 on Monday. There was an attitude among editors: 'Look, we're going to war, why do we even worry about all this contrary stuff?'"[24]

Post executive editor Leonard Downie Jr. admitted, "We were so focused on trying to figure out what the Administration was doing that we were not giving the same play to people who said it wouldn't be a good idea to go to war and were questioning the Administration's rationale. Not enough of those stories were put on the front page. That was a mistake on my part." Across the country, "the voices raising questions about the war were lonely ones," Downie said. "We didn't pay enough attention to the minority."[24]

Downie and his fellow editors at the *Post* were typical of the media echo chamber. They all shut down or drowned out the voices of the enlightened minority in order to preserve their storyline. In the meantime, they gullibly and shamefully echoed the Administration's sales pitch for war.

The Echo Chamber and National Security

During the World Wars and the Cold War, the government feared the media would undermine national security by leaking state secrets. In the lead up to the Iraq War, the media did indeed undermine national security—not by defying the government's wishes but by going along with them. The media not only allowed the Administration to sell the Iraq War, it also promoted the war by echoing the sales pitch. After 30,000 American casualties, the Iraq War still has no end in sight and every potential foe on earth knows the American military is stretched to the limit for the foreseeable future. Thanks in large part to the media, America's national security has never been so imperiled.

CHAPTER THREE
LIPSTICK ON A PIG: THE IRAQ WAR COVERAGE

"You can put lipstick on a pig, but it's still a pig."
Torie Clarke, Assistant Secretary of Defense
for Public Affairs during the Iraq War

"Information War" on Al Jazeera

The Iraq War obliterated whatever lines once divided combat, entertainment, and journalism. The military trained America's war correspondents and then "embedded" them in combat units. Networks hired former military officers to add color commentary to their news coverage. The military staged phony combat operations so their own film crews could capture the action and feed edited footage to a fawning media. Lt. Col. Rick Long, head of media relations for the U.S. Marine Corps, explained that the Pentagon's media strategy was an essential part of its war strategy, "Frankly, our job is to win the war. Part of that is information warfare.

So we are going to attempt to dominate the information environment."[1]

This "information war" against the media may have also slipped down a slippery slope into actual combat. In Afghanistan, an American missile destroyed Al Jazeera's office in Kabul. Former British Home Secretary David Blunkett advised Prime Minister Tony Blair in late March 2003 to bomb the Al Jazeera television transmitter in Baghdad. "There wasn't a worry from me," Blunkett later explained, "because I believed that this was a war and in a war you wouldn't allow the broadcast to continue taking place." A month later, a U.S. missile hit Al Jazeera's office in Baghdad, killing reporter Tareq Ayyoub and wounding another staff member.

During the Marines' April 2004 assault on Fallujah, American cameras obeyed the Pentagon and stayed away while Al Jazeera provided harrowing video of civilian casualties from inside the city. Rumsfeld condemned Al Jazeera's coverage as "vicious, inaccurate and inexcusable." The next day at a White House meeting, according to Britain's *Daily Mail,* the AP, and the *Washington Post,* George Bush discussed bombing Al Jazeera's Qatar headquarters with Tony Blair.[2] A senior British diplomat noted Bush's bombing plan in a memo that was later leaked. The British press gave extensive coverage to the story; the American media mostly ignored it. Some speculate that Bush must have been "joking" about bombing Al Jazeera. Maybe so, but no other news network had their offices bombed twice, in both Afghanistan and Baghdad.

"Mascots for the Military"

The Defense Department controlled media coverage during the 1991 Gulf War by restricting the movements of the war correspondents and spoon-feeding them filtered information. During the planning of the 2003 Operation Iraqi Freedom, Torie Clarke, the Assistant Secretary of Defense for Public Affairs, came up with the idea of shaping media coverage by embedding journalists in combat units. Clarke, who'd previously served as president of a major advertising firm and was vice president of the National Cable Telecommunications Association, boasted about this stroke of marketing genius in her aptly titled 2006 book, *Lipstick on a Pig*.

By March 2003, when Bush launched the invasion of Iraq, about 775 reporters and photographers signed contracts with the military to become "embeds." According to their contracts, journalists were limited in what they were allowed to report and had to undergo training in military boot camps. Boot camps always serve two functions: preparing recruits for the dangers of combat and indoctrinating them with the military ethos. The embedded journalists emerged from their training with an *esprit de corps* that swelled when they joined their assigned units and saw action together.

Gina Cavallaro, a reporter for the *Army Times* said, "They're [the journalists] relying more on the military to get them where they want to go, and as a result, the military is getting smarter about getting its own story told." The embeds were in bed with the military. They were also at the mercy of the military that could cut off access as punishment for deviating from the Pentagon's storyline.

Two embedded journalists from the *Virginian-Pilot* newspaper lost their credentials after they had the temerity to publish a picture of a bullet-ridden Humvee parked in a Kuwaiti camp. Embedded journalists quickly got the message: "If you deviate from the storyline, you go home." Legendary journalist Gay Talese described the new relationship between the military and the embeds, "Those correspondents who drive around in tanks and armored personnel carriers are spoon-fed what the military gives them and they become *mascots for the military*."[3]

Shock and Awe

On the first day of the invasion, the storyline blazed across America's television screens through graphic banners that literally framed the war news. Some banners came from the Pentagon PR machine: *Shock and Awe* and *Operation Iraqi Freedom*. Other catch phrases were generated by the individual news departments: CNN's *America's New War*, NBC's *America at War*, and MSNBC's *Countdown: Iraq*.

The storyline was simple. The United States was going to use its vast technological superiority to destroy a dastardly dictator and liberate the Iraqi people. The *New York Times* described the news coverage of the first day of the war, "'Shock and awe' should be the code name for the Pentagon's media strategy. The first full day of television coverage of the invasion of Iraq revealed not the fog of war but a firestorm of amazing combat images." It continued, "From Navy fighter jets roaring off the deck of the carrier Constellation to grainy, green night-scope glimpses of American tanks moving across the Kuwaiti border into Iraq, television showed more live military action in one day than in the entire 1991 war."[4]

On the evening news programs, Americans watched the kind of war against Iraq that they had become accustomed to since the early 1990s. TV cameras mounted on the top of a Baghdad hotel captured explosions from American bombs and cruise missiles that lit up the sky. Seen from the vantage point of a long lens shot, these explosions were reminiscent of an episode of the 1980s TV show, *The A-Team*—lots of guns firing and bombs exploding but no one ever gets hurt. Of course, the reality of bombing a city of six million was not so benign. While Americans saw a bloodless war, Al Jazeera broadcast the carnage throughout the Arab world.

According to the *New York Times,* European networks like the BBC exposed their audiences to the pain of war by training their cameras on refugees fleeing their homes. But "American television was more focused on dazzling combat images and the human side of the nation's warriors. By agreeing to give hundreds of journalists [embeds] front-row seats, the Defense Department hoped to get reporters and viewers rooting for the visiting team on the first day out."[5]

Along with the pro-war imagery, a review of the six television networks and news channels found on-camera commentary in the first three weeks of the war was overwhelmingly pro-war. Nearly two-thirds of all commentators (sixty-four percent) favored the war and only ten percent opposed it. American viewers were more than six times as likely to see a pro-war commentator as one who was anti-war. The American media tended to chose anti-war commentators who were foreigners, and for every twenty-five American commentators who favored the war, there was only one American voice against it. By cherry picking the commentators, the media gave viewers the impression that opponents of the war were a tiny fringe with questionable allegiance to the United States.[6]

Wes Clarke: General-for-Hire

While the Pentagon embedded journalists in the military, military men became embedded in the media. Television networks hired former generals to comment on the war. In the early days of the war, these generals-for-hire consistently reinforced the media's storyline about how America's technical superiority was going to shock and awe the Iraqis into submission. In a typical comment, CNN's Wes Clarke told Wolf Blitzer on April 6, 2003, "Well, the United States has very, very important technological advantages. Unlike previous efforts in urban combat, we control the skies." While the embedded journalists became "mascots for the military," Wes Clarke and the other TV generals were 'homers,' providing color commentary that was constantly—and authoritatively—pro-war. "First of all, I think the troops and all the people over there, the commanders, have done an absolutely superb job, a sensational job." Clarke crowed, "And I think the results speak for themselves."[7]

Jessica "Rambo" Lynch

Weeks after *Shock and Awe*'s universally acclaimed blockbuster opening, the media's celebratory storyline began to run up against reality.

March 23rd: Dozens of Americans killed or injured in an ambush in Nasiriya.

March 24th: Saddam gives a twenty-five-minute televised speech taunting the Americans.

March 27th: Iraqis in civilian clothes and suicide bombers kill dozens of Americans; U.S. troops accidentally shoot up a van full of women and children.

March 30th: Don Rumsfeld and the Chairman of the Joint Chiefs, General Richard Meyers, have to go on the talk show circuit to reassure the public that the troops are not stretched too thin.[8]

The Pentagon and the gung-ho media needed a new story that fit the *Shock and Awe* storyline. Within days, the Pentagon discovered a starlet named Jessica Lynch and the media got its blockbuster.

In the early morning of April 2, 2003, the Pentagon's communications team woke up the press at the media center in Qatar to announce the dramatic rescue of the Iraq War's first hero, a nineteen-year-old girl from the hills of West Virginia. Jessica Lynch had been riding in a supply convoy which took a wrong turn and was ambushed near Nassiriya.

According to the first media reports, Lynch became a real life Rambo during the ambush, firing at the Iraqis even after she sustained multiple gunshot wounds and watched several other soldiers in her unit die at her feet.[9] The *Washington Post*'s article "She Was Fighting to the Death" was typical of the coverage. Like Judy Miller's reporting on Saddam's WMD, the *Post*'s report on Lynch was based on a mysterious unnamed official, "'She was fighting to the death,' the official said. 'She did not want to be taken alive.'" The *Post* also reported this official's claims that Lynch was "stabbed when Iraqi forces closed in on her position."

Who was the official who gave the *Post* this dramatic story? Why couldn't he or she be identified? Buried in the *Post*'s exciting report was one caveat, "Several officials cautioned that the precise sequence of events is still being determined, and that further information will emerge as Lynch is debriefed....

Pentagon officials said they had heard 'rumors' of Lynch's heroics but had no confirmation." So the *Washington Post*, along with the rest of the media, ran the exciting tale of Lynch "fighting to the death" based on an unnamed source and despite warnings from military officials that all the talk of Lynch's heroic fight was based on rumors. The story of little Jessica's last stand, however, was too good to pass up because of something passé like "journalistic ethics."

The only thing more dramatic than Lynch's last stand was the story of her rescue. The Pentagon claimed Lynch was interrogated and slapped while in the hospital. A courageous Iraqi lawyer, Mohammed Odeh Al Rehaief, was so appalled at her treatment that he risked his life to inform the Americans where Lynch was being held. Just after midnight, Army Rangers and Navy Seals stormed the Nassiriya hospital where they doggedly searched for Lynch despite coming under fire from Iraqi guards. Not only did the military have a dramatic feel-good story for the media, but they also had a five-minute video of the "daring" rescue shot in the creepy green glow of a night-vision camera and edited by the military PR unit. The media took the bait, and Americans watched a constant replay of the dramatic video over the subsequent week.

The reality of the Jessica Lynch story was a lot less exciting, but a lot more revealing. Rather than making a dramatic stand against the Iraqi ambush, Lynch had been knocked unconscious when her truck slammed into another American vehicle. The Iraqis who discovered the unconscious Lynch did not shoot or stab her; they took her to the nearest hospital where she spent eight days in recovery.

Iraqi doctors provided Lynch with the best treatment they could in the middle of a war. "We gave her three bottles of blood, two of them from the medical staff because there was no blood at this time," said Dr. Harith al-Houssona, Lynch's primary physician. Lynch was given the only specialist bed in the hospital and was attended by one of only two nurses on the entire floor. The nurse later recalled, "I was like a mother to her and she was like a daughter." Lynch had a broken arm, a broken thigh, and a dislocated ankle. "There was no [sign of] shooting, no bullet inside her body, no stab wound—only RTA, road traffic accident," her doctor recalled. Lynch was not shot or stabbed, and she later denied firing her weapon at all. "They [the Americans] want to distort the picture," her doctor complained, "I don't know why they think there is some benefit in saying she has a bullet injury."

Two days before Lynch's "rescue," her doctor arranged for an ambulance to deliver her back to U.S. forces, but U.S. troops opened fire when the ambulance with Jessica inside approached an American checkpoint. The ambulance returned her to the hospital.

The facts of the actual rescue also turned out to be wildly inaccurate. U.S. troops faced absolutely no resistance. The only shots fired around the hospital came from American guns. When the rescue team burst into the hospital, they began breaking down doors in the intensive care unit looking for Lynch but could have just asked one of the staff where she was. One soldier put a gun to Lynch's orthopedist's head while others restrained a couple of doctors and a patient. Jessica's doctor said the scene reminded him of a Hollywood movie, "They cry, 'Go, Go, Go!' and shout 'Go, Go, Go!' with guns and blanks without bullets. Blanks and sounds of explosions and break down the door. We were very scared. They made a show—an action movie like Sylvester Stallone or Jackie Chan with jumping and shouting, breaking down doors."[10]

The rescuers were indeed making a movie. Along with the troops was the military's camera crew, which later edited the raw footage in time for the big press announcement of Lynch's rescue. The television media, of course, loved the dramatic video and replayed it constantly over the subsequent days. The BBC later asked the Pentagon to release the full tape of the rescue to clear up the many discrepancies between the Iraqi witnesses and American rescuers. The Pentagon refused.

Within a week, 600 stories appeared about Lynch's heroic stand and her dramatic rescue. Her largely fictional story dominated the war news, drowning out reports of mounting casualties and a slowed advance. Lynch was offered a $1 million book deal, and MTV asked her to host a TV show. NBC even prepared a made-for-TV movie titled *Saving Private Lynch,* a riff on Steven Spielberg's hit *Saving Private Ryan. Variety* praised the Lynch movie, *"Mission Impossible* but true." The Iraqi lawyer who tipped off the military to her location also got in on the action with a $500,000 book deal and a guest spot on *Oprah.*

The Pentagon's story started to unravel less than two weeks later and news organizations like ABC News and the *Washington Post* began offering corrections and more accurate versions of the events. The *Post* ran its less dramatic version on A17, but by then fiction had already become fact. The *Washington Post* Ombudsman noted that the tale "didn't get knocked down until it didn't matter so much anymore."[11]

John MacArthur, editor of *Harper's,* put it best, "In America it doesn't matter anymore what is right or wrong. The public is conditioned to believe everything: no matter if it is emotional stories or lies on weapons of mass destruction."[12]

Saddam's Statue

A week after the military and the media collaborated on the phony but sufficiently distracting Jessica Lynch story, they came up with another show. On April 9, 2003, the Marines came upon Firdos Square in central Baghdad, the site of a forty-foot statue of Saddam Hussein, and a Marine colonel got the inspiration to pull down the statue with a tank recovery vehicle. Marines began a dramatic show for the media cameras by draping an American flag over the statue's head, but a member of the military's psychological warfare unit intervened and told the Marines to remove the Stars and Stripes.

"God bless them," the Psy-Ops officer recalled, "but we were thinking...that this was just bad news. We didn't want to look like an occupation force, and some of the Iraqis were saying, 'No, we want an Iraqi flag!'" The Psy-Ops team then transformed the scene into a seemingly spontaneous Iraqi undertaking. Using loudspeakers, Psy-Ops agents summoned Iraqi civilians to the square and picked up a few Iraqi kids and placed them on the tank recovery vehicle.[13]

Once the crowd gathered around the statue, news cameras in the square began beaming live images of Iraqi civilians cheering as the Marines pulled down the statue and then jumped on its pieces. None of the networks offered viewers a wide shot which would have shown the large square almost deserted except for a small crowd gathered by Psy-Ops at the base of the statue.

Two days later, on ABC's *Nightline,* Robert Krulwich pointed out the deceptive camera angle, "On television, the crowd gathered around the statue seemed, well, big. But on TV, framing is everything. Widen the frame of this scene and look. It's kind of empty in the foreground. Now pull back further, this is about three minutes after the statue fell, and that big celebration seen all over the world wasn't really very big. Pictures on TV can deceive, same with pictures in the paper."[14] But a wide frame shot would have deviated from the dramatic storyline. The media was expected to deliver video of grateful, happy Iraqi crowds cheering U.S. soldiers like Paris in 1944. That's what Dick Cheney promised.

Even though the crowd around Saddam's statue was neither large nor spontaneous, the media went along with the show. The *New York Times* reported that "thousands" of "ordinary Iraqis" took part in the statue-toppling and the *Washington Post* described the scene as "reminiscent of the fall of the Berlin Wall in 1989" when tens of thousands participated.[15]

The so-called "iconic images" of the toppled statue were plastered on the front page of every major newspaper and played repeatedly on TV along with commentary like *Washington Post* reporter Ceci Connolly appearing on Fox News: "It was reminiscent, I think, of the Berlin Wall. And just sort of that pure emotional expression, not choreographed, not stage-managed, the way so many things these days seem to be—really breathtaking."[16]

The news coverage of the falling statue also gave millions of Americans the false notion that the war was over. Although the fighting was still heavy, the financial markets suddenly improved. According to the UPI, investors on Wall Street "applauded images of a statue of Saddam...[which] sent stocks surging...."[17]

Mission Accomplished

A month later, the military, the media, and the White House PR team collaborated on another made-for-TV extravaganza to officially mark the end of the war. On May 1, 2003, Bush flew in a Lockheed S-3 Viking and landed on the *U.S.S. Abraham Lincoln,* an aircraft carrier returning from combat operations in the Persian Gulf. The scene was reminiscent of Vladimir Putin's flight to Chechnya in a fighter jet during Russia's war against the Chechen rebels a few years earlier. Images of Putin strutting around in his flight suit filled the Russian media and helped get him elected in 2000. Karl Rove no doubt thought Bush's carrier landing would generate great images for the 2004 reelection bid.

Bush wanted to fly in a fighter jet like Putin but was prevented by the Secret Service. Instead, he was flown in a refueling plane decorated with the legend "George W. Bush Commander in Chief." Bush hopped out of the jet in a full flight suit and tucked his helmet under his arm, looking like a character from the 1980s movie *Top Gun.* No other sitting American president had ever worn a military uniform out of respect for the traditional divide between the military and its civilian leadership. MSNBC's Chris Matthews loved Bush's fashion statement, "Here's a president who's really nonverbal. He's like Eisenhower. He looks great in a military uniform."

When asked if he flew the jet, Bush said, "Yes, I flew it. I miss flying I can tell you that."[18] MSNBC's

Chris Matthews knew Bush was just a passenger, but it didn't matter: "The president there—look at this guy! We're watching him. He looks like he flew the plane. He only flew it as a passenger, but he's flown.... He looks for real. What is it about the Commander in Chief role, the hat that he does wear that makes him, I mean, he seems like—he didn't fight in a war, but he looks like he does." Bush wasn't a war hero but he played one on TV.

For Matthews, like most of media, image was reality. "What does that image mean to the American people? A guy who can actually get into a supersonic plane and actually fly in an unpressurized cabin like an actual jet pilot?"

Initially the White House claimed that Bush had to arrive in the jet instead of a helicopter because the carrier was too far out to sea. In reality, the *U.S.S. Abraham Lincoln* was so near the California coast that TV cameras onboard could have broadcast shots of the San Diego skyline if they were pointed in the right direction.[19] But like the ballyhooed fall of Saddam's stature, the media didn't want any camera shots that would deviate from the spectacular storyline.

After changing into a business suit, Bush emerged a few hours later (primetime on the East coast) to deliver a speech surrounded by the carrier crew under a White House-produced banner declaring "Mission Accomplished." The speech was timed for the "magic hour" when cinematographers like to shoot outdoor scenes because the sun casts a flattering glow. The *U.S.S. Abraham Lincoln's* return to port was even delayed a day so that Bush could give his speech on Thursday—the most watched night on television. It was "Must-See TV."

The media commentary fed the phony drama. CNN's Lou Dobbs said, "[Bush] looked alternatively like a Commander in Chief, rock star, movie star, and one of the guys."[20]

Fox News's Mort Kondracke called the carrier landing "fantastic theater" and likened it to the Hollywood blockbuster *Independence Day* in which the President of the United States flies combat missions against invading aliens.

MSNBC's Chris Matthews described "the president looking very much like a jet, you know, a high-flying jet star."

David Broder of the *Washington Post* marveled on *Meet the Press* about Bush's physical posture, "This president has learned how to move in a way that just conveys a great sense of authority and command."

ABC's nightly news coverage featured Bob Woodruff intoning, "It was an impressive sight from the deck of the *Abraham Lincoln*. This wartime president soaring overhead and then coming in at about 150 miles an hour. The first sitting president to land on a carrier." Unfortunately for Bob Woodruff, the "Mission Accomplished" banner turned out to be tragically overoptimistic. Almost three years later, Woodruff was seriously injured in Iraq by an IED while covering the enduring war that claimed 3,800 American lives AFTER Bush's "Mission Accomplished" moment on the *U.S.S. Abraham Lincoln*.

Chris Matthews and the Great Media Flip-Flop

On the night of Bush's *Top Gun* photo-op, MSNBC'S Chris Matthews could not contain his rapture over the "president's amazing display of leadership tonight.... The president deserves everything he's doing tonight in terms of his leadership," Matthews observed. "He won the war. He was an effective commander. Everybody recognizes that, I believe, except a few critics.... If you're going to run against him, you'd better be ready to take [that] away from him."

Matthew's guest, right wing pundit Ann Coulter seconded the notion that the images from the carrier were political gold. "It's stunning. It's amazing. I think it's huge. I mean, he's landing on a boat at 150 miles per hour. It's tremendous. It's hard to imagine any Democrat being able to do that. And it doesn't matter if Democrats try to ridicule it. It's stunning, and it speaks for itself."

Later that day, Matthews appeared on MSNBC's *Countdown with Keith Olbermann* to glorify Bush some more, "We're proud of our president. Americans love having a *guy* as president, a guy who has a little swagger, who's physical, who's not a complicated guy like [former President Bill] Clinton or even like [former Democratic presidential candidates Michael] Dukakis or [Walter] Mondale, all those guys, [George] McGovern. They want a guy who's president. Women like a guy who's president. Check it out. The women like this war." So women "like this war" because Bush made it sexy by not being complicated and effete like the Democrats? Matthews often makes strange statements, but even for him that's bizarre.

Matthews went on, "I think we like having a hero as our president. It's simple. We're not like the Brits. We don't want an indoor prime minister type, or the Danes or the Dutch or the Italians, or a Putin. Can you imagine Putin getting elected here? We want a guy as president."[21] But unlike Bush, Putin really did fly the jet.

In 2004, Matthews and much of the media criticized John Kerry for being a "flip-flopper," but within a couple of years, the *Hardball* host and many of his fellow talking heads committed the biggest flip-flop in American history when they turned on Bush and his war. Matthews' recent cynicism toward Bush and the Iraq War has nothing to do with some sort of epiphany. Like the rest of the talking heads who suddenly jumped on the Bush-bashing bandwagon, he feared that his ratings would follow Bush's approval ratings into the toilet. And like everyone in the media who were once cheerleaders for Bush and the disastrous Iraq War because it grabbed ratings and headlines, Matthews' career has not been hurt by this stunning flip-flop.

Judy Miller Finds Saddam's WMDs

The failure to find any WMDs presented a big problem for the Administration and the media. How could the United States have started a war over non-existent WMDs? How could the media have been so supportive of the Administration's false storyline? Wouldn't the American public demand a full accounting of the failures of the government and the media? But Judith Miller once again offered a farfetched report that supported the WMD storyline.

Miller was embedded with a military team hunting for unconventional weapons in Iraq. In a front page *New York Times* article titled "After Effects: Prohibited Weapons; Illicit Arms Kept Till Eve of War, An Iraqi Scientist is Said to Assert,"[22] she claimed that although her military team did not find any WMDs, they did find an unidentified scientist who revealed that Saddam had lots of WMDs after all. Where did they go? Miller repeated the scientist's fantastic story about how Saddam destroyed all his chemical weapons and biological warfare equipment "only days before the war began." She also asserted, "Iraq had secretly sent unconventional weapons and technology to Syria, starting in the mid-1990s, and that more recently Iraq was cooperating with Al Qaeda." Not coincidently, Bush Administration officials had just begun offering the same explanations for the absence of WMDs.

The idea that massive stockpiles of deadly weapons could be completely destroyed in "days" is absurd and would have raised the suspicions of a real journalist, but Miller just repeated the lies. According to Miller, the military would not identify the scientist because they supposedly "feared he might be subject to reprisals." She also revealed that the WMD search team refused to allow her to interview the scientist,

"Under the terms of her accreditation to report on the activities of MET Alpha, this reporter was not permitted to interview the scientist or visit his home." She even dutifully "submitted a copy of her article to the military officials who deleted certain details." Given the military's censorship and their refusal to allow Miller to speak with the scientist who made the absurd claim about Saddam destroying all his WMDs in days, one might think she'd be suspicious about the information that the military was giving her. But Miller explained, "You have to accept terms to get to be an embed with a unit like MET Alpha. No reporter could have gone with them without agreeing to protect the unit's work and not expose them or their sources to danger."

And so without any independent confirmation, Miller took the word of the military and repeated a second-hand account of an unidentified scientist's absurd claims. Once again, the *New York Times* abrogated journalistic standards and knowingly ran one of her absurd stories.

Miller and her editors were as invested in the existence of Saddam's WMDs as any official in the Bush Administration. At the start of the war, Miller's career was riding high based on her reporting about Saddam's WMDs. Now the failure to find WMDs threatened her career and the credibility of the *New York Times.* So Miller endorsed the Administration's explanations for the missing WMDs and the *Times* had no problem going along with it. "The officials' account of the scientist's assertions and the discovery of the buried material, which they described as the most important discovery to date in the hunt for illegal weapons, supports the Bush Administration's charges that Iraq continued to develop those weapons and lied to the United Nations about it.... The officials' accounts also provided an explanation for why United States forces had not yet turned up banned weapons in Iraq."

In other words, Judith Miller and her friends in the Administration were right about the WMDs after all. Saddam must have conveniently destroyed them just before U.S. troops arrived.

The New WMD Storyline

The media began to echo and thereby reinforce Miller's cover story. "Reporter Judith Miller of the *New York Times* does believe the weapons are there," Fox News' Bill O'Reilly declared, "She spelled out the weapons yesterday."

Rush Limbaugh devoted a portion of his radio show to Miller's "big, huge, very important story" and wrote on his website, "If this appeared anywhere other than the sainted *New York Times,* many liberals would be out there pooh-poohing it. Since it appears there, what are they going to say?"

The next day, Miller confronted some skepticism from *PBS NewsHour*'s Ray Suarez, "Has the unit you've been traveling with found any evidence of weapons of mass destruction in Iraq?"

Miller was confident, "Well, I think they found something more than a smoking gun. What they've found is a silver bullet in the form of a person, an Iraqi individual, a scientist, as we've called him, who really worked on the programs, who knows them, firsthand, and who has led MET Alpha people to some pretty startling conclusions." In other words, forget the *smoking gun* in the form of a *mushroom cloud,* the military found something better—a *silver bullet* in a form of a *scientist!*

Suarez tried to bring the conversation back to the realm of sanity, "But those stockpiles that we've heard about?"

Miller deflected, "Well, those have either been destroyed by Saddam Hussein, according to the *scientists,* or they have been shipped to Syria for safekeeping." Notice how the one "scientist" in Miller's original story suddenly became scientists (plural). "And that's what the Bush Administration has finally done. They have changed the political environment, and they've enabled people like the *scientists* that MET Alpha has found to come forth."

Miller's shoddy reporting and exaggerations about "scientists" coming forward to explain the disappearance of Saddam's WMDs began to be repeated in the media. The echo chamber welcomed any news that supported the original storyline. For example Paul Leventhal of the Nuclear Control Institute told MSNBC, "The scientists told the *New York Times* that they had buried the chemical weapons."[23]

Over the subsequent weeks, talking heads started to repeat Miller's claims that the military found the "smoking gun" or "silver bullet" or "scientists" proving the existence of WMDs. Soon poll numbers showed that a majority of Americans believed the military did find WMDs. Just like the big lie about Saddam's ties to Al Qaeda, Saddam's WMDs became fact through repetition in the media.

To this day, no accounting has been made for how the American media and the Bush Administration got the WMD story so terribly wrong and pushed the United States into an unnecessary war that has killed 150,000 Iraqis, destroyed tens of thousands of

American lives, and cost a trillion dollars. Just a few years later, this failure of the media and the Congress to expose the lies and punish the culprits allowed Bush to take the United States to the brink of an even more disastrous war.

CHAPTER FOUR

AHMADINEJAD: AMERICA'S NEXT TOP BOOGEYMAN

*"There's an old saying in Tennessee—
I know it's in Texas, probably in Tennessee—
that says fool me once, shame on—shame on you.
Fool me—you can't get fooled again."*
George W. Bush, Nashville, Tennessee 2002

By 2007, everyone knew the Bush Administration repeatedly fooled the media on the two biggest stories of the twenty-first century: 9/11 and Iraq. Yet the media coverage on Iran again echoed the Administration's hype, hysteria, and lies and collaborated in bringing America to the brink of another fiasco.

Iran: Axis or Ally?

The hyping of the Iranian threat began when Bush labeled Iran part of the "Axis of Evil" during his 2002 State of the Union address. The media immediately embraced the phrase because it fit the 9/11 storyline—the world neatly divided between good and evil with the United States on "the side of angels" in a fight against the "Islamo Fascist" evildoers. As always, reality was much more complicated than this easy storyline.

In fact, Iran was a great enemy of the perpetrators of 9/11 long before 2001. Iran waged a covert war against the Taliban and Wahabi-Sunni terrorist networks like Al Qaeda in the 1990s. While George Bush gave economic aid to the repressive Taliban in early 2001, Iran was funding the Taliban's bitter enemies, the Northern Alliance. Immediately after 9/11, Iran provided the United States with key intelligence about Afghanistan and helped the Defense Department establish ties with the Northern Alliance, which drove the Taliban from Kabul two months later. The Iranians were willing to continue assisting America's war against both the Taliban and Al Qaeda in the winter of 2001, but Bush and the neo-cons ignored the advice of the State Department and CIA and spurned further Iranian assistance.

Once Bush deployed the Axis of Evil line in January 2002, there was no turning back. Our leaders missed a great opportunity to learn from the Iranians and build ties between our intelligence communities that might have helped us find bin Laden. Of course, Administration ideologues did not want such cooperation. They had already begun to redirect public anger and anxiety about 9/11 toward Iraq and Iran. The media echo chamber facilitated this bait and switch by cheering the simplistic, inaccurate Axis of Evil trope. Thanks to neo-con ideologues and a gullible, lazy media, the United States blew a great opportunity to work with the Iranians to destroy our common enemy: the Al Qaeda. Instead, the U.S. formed a strategic partnership with Pakistan, Iran's regional competitor and a longtime ally of the Taliban. Bin Laden now remains safe in a Pakistani sanctuary out of the reach of U.S. forces in Afghanistan.

Enter Ahmadinejad

America's invasion of Iraq and Bush's belligerent rhetoric toward Iran also helped undermine the reform movement of two-term Iranian President Akbar Hashemi Rafsanjani. In 2005, religious conservative Mahmoud Ahmadinejad rode a wave of anti-American anxiety to victory in the Iranian presidential elections.

Ahmadinejad was straight out of central casting for the role of anti-American bad guy and played the perfect foil for George Bush. Both men possess an ignorant Manichean worldview combined with a careless penchant for provocative rhetoric. Ahmadinejad's stated wish to see Israel "wiped off the map" may have been a mistranslation, but his sentiment was clear and threatening. His suggestion that the Holocaust was a myth alienated even the most open-minded Americans.

Ahmadinejad is obviously not a force for peace, but the threat he might pose is limited. The President of Iran is not that country's highest authority. The Supreme Ruler and the religious mullahs make all the big decisions. The American media downplayed this fact in their Ahmadinejad coverage because their storyline called for a new threatening villain to play Bush's nemesis.

By 2005, the echo chamber had two characters that perfectly fit the U.S. vs. Iran storyline—a cowboy president spoiling for a cinematic showdown with America's latest boogeyman. The media was primed for exploitation by anyone who wanted to see war between the U.S. and Iran.

Iran Hostage Replay

Shortly after Ahmadinejad's election, Iran Focus, a London-based Iranian dissident group, claimed they had a photograph of Ahmadinejad guarding an American hostage during the 1979-1981 U.S.

embassy takeover. Iran Focus was also known to be the public relations branch of People's Mujahedin of Iran (PMOI). The State Department labeled PMOI a terrorist organization, and Saddam Hussein had sponsored it in a covert war against Iran. Ahmadinejad did not really look like the man in the photo except for a similarly trimmed beard, but the media embraced the story because it fit the storyline. The major Western news agencies—AP, Reuters, and AFP—ran the photo along with Iran Focus' unsubstantiated allegations. This was the same kind of lazy journalism that allowed Chalabi's Iraqi dissident group to use the American media to disseminate stories about Saddam's WMDs via Judith Miller and others.

The White House echoed speculation that Ahmadinejad was one of the embassy hostage-takers. Bush spokesman Scott McClellan said the U.S. government took the allegations seriously and was "looking into them to better understand the facts."

State Department spokesman Sean McCormack declared, "We, as a government, are working to establish the facts surrounding this story. But I do want to say one thing and that is to underscore the fact that we have not forgotten—we have not forgotten—the fact that fifty-one of our diplomats were held for 444 days, that they were taken hostage."[1]

Bush told reporters he had "no information, but obviously his involvement raises many questions."[2] Notice that although Bush admitted having "no information," he did not hesitate to mention Ahmadinejad's "involvement" in the hostage crisis.

Ahmadinejad denied he was in the photo and leaders of the 1979 embassy take-over affirmed that he did not participate and initially opposed it. (The CIA later confirmed the Iranian president's denials.) But the echo chamber gave credence to former hostages who attested to Ahmadinejad involvement based solely on twenty-eight-year-old memories. "As soon as I saw the face, it rang a lot of bells to me," said former hostage Don Sharer. "Take twenty years off of him. He was there. He was there in the background, more like an adviser." Sharer told NBC he was reading the *Indianapolis Star* and "all of a sudden, up pops the devil, right in front of me." The *International Herald Tribune,* owned by the *New York Times,* ended its report on the photo with a typical Sharer quote, "All I can say is I remember the fellow being very cruel-like, stern, a very narrow, beady-eyed character."[3]

CNN quoted former hostage William Daugherty, "I saw [Ahmadinejad's] picture in the *Washington Post* on Saturday morning, recognized it immediately and then sent an e-mail out to some of my former colleagues...telling them what I thought and seeing what kind of responses they might have to it." CNN reported Daugherty's memory of Ahmadinejad "acting in a supervisory or leadership capacity during the first...two and a half weeks, [but] on the nineteenth day, I was moved into solitary confinement and had limited contact with even my Iranian guards after that."[4] Daugherty's twenty-eight-year-old memories were suspiciously detailed, but CNN echoed them anyway.

Army attaché Colonel Charles Scott said he remembered Ahmadinejad calling the Americans "pigs and dogs and we deserved to be locked up forever." Possibly suspecting that his own account was too detailed to be credible, Scott explained, "When you're placed in a life-threatening situation of that nature, you just remember those things."

The *Washington Times* repeated Scott's claim that Ahmadinejad told a guard, "You shouldn't let these pigs out of their cells," and quoted Scott on Ahmadinejad, "He was one of the top two or three leaders; the new president of Iran is a terrorist." The hyperbole of these old memories should have raised red flags among reporters, but the major news organizations echoed accusations about the "beady-eyed" Ahmadinejad because they fit the storyline.

One exception to the echo chamber's embrace of this storyline was Joel Brinkley of *New York Times*. Although Brinkley quoted extensively from Scott and Sharer, he mentioned at the very end of the article that the former hostages were plaintiffs in several lawsuits that unsuccessfully sought compensation from the Iranian government. Brinkley noted that Congress could still pass legislation allowing Scott and Sharer to revive their legal gambit. At the end of the article, he slyly quoted an e-mail exchange between two of the oft-quoted witnesses, "William Daugherty asked, 'Does this provide any additional leverage for you all in terms of the Bush Administration's unwillingness to go along with any compensation?'"[5] Brinkley's implication was subtle but clear: the memories of these former hostages may have had political and financial motives. The rest of the media, however, avoided this angle.

Iran's Nukes

The 2007 National Intelligence Estimate revealed that the Iranians shut down their nuclear program in 2003. But from 2004 until the release of the NIE three years later, the Bush Administration repeatedly claimed with certainty that Iran had a nuclear program. The media did not investigate. It merely echoed the certitude that Iran had an ongoing nuclear weapons program. A front-page *New York Times* story on June 27, 2005, mentioned that China might block "efforts to bring the issue of Iran's nuclear weapons program before the United Nations Security Council."[6]

Another *Times* front-pager by Michael Gordon (October 19, 2004), suggested that a U.S.-friendly regime in Iraq might pressure "Iran to halt its nuclear weapons program."[7] And a *Times* article (March 26, 2005), noted that a government report found "grave weaknesses remained in efforts to track Iranian and North Korean nuclear programs."[8] Of course the *New York Times* wasn't the only news outlet to confuse unsubstantiated charges with facts. A 2005 *Newsweek* article, presumptuously titled "Iran's Nuclear Lies," parroted the White House storyline and failed to inform readers that the International Atomic Energy Agency found no evidence that Iran was lying at all.[9] Since the White House said Iran had an ongoing nuclear weapons program, the media took the program as a given.

A good example of how the echo chamber followed the Bush storyline is an April 2007 AP story titled "Iran Expands Uranium Enrichment Effort." The article made a big deal of Iran's announcement that it began enriching uranium with 3,000 centrifuges. "Defiantly expanding a nuclear program that has drawn U.N. sanctions and condemnation from the West.... Uranium enrichment can produce fuel for a nuclear reactor or the material for a nuclear warhead," the AP observed.[10] The article then quotes condemnations from a U.S. State Department spokesman and a White House official, a "no comment" from the IAEA, and some inflammatory quotes from Ahmadinejad. After all the rhetoric and accusations, the article finally reveals in its twenty-second paragraph that Iran's 3,000 centrifuges were actually insignificant, "Experts say the Natanz plant needs between 50,000 to 60,000 centrifuges to consistently produce fuel for a reactor or build a warhead." So in the twenty-second paragraph of a twenty-eight-paragraph story, we're told Iran's 3,000 centrifuges are one-twentieth of the number experts say are necessary to build a nuclear bomb.[11]

Like all the talk about Saddam's WMDs, the ubiquitous reports about Iran's nuclear program convinced a majority of Americans that it existed beyond a doubt. A *Los Angeles Times/Bloomberg* poll from June 2006 asked, "Do you approve or disapprove of the way George W. Bush is handling the situation with Iran's nuclear weapons program?"

Forty percent approved and thirty-one percent disapproved, but all seemed to agree that there was a nuclear weapons program.

The poll also asked, "Do you think Iran will be stopped from getting nuclear weapons through diplomatic solutions, or only through military action, or do you think Iran will eventually get nuclear weapons?" Fifty-six percent said Iran would only be stopped through military action. When asked, "If Iran continues to produce material that can be used to develop nuclear weapons, would you support or oppose the U.S. taking military action against Iran?" Fifty-two percent said yes, they would support military action.

A Fox News poll asked, "Do you believe Iran's nuclear program is for peaceful purposes or military purposes?" Eighty percent said military. "Do you believe the United States should take a softer line with Iran, including more diplomacy, or take a tougher line, including military action if necessary?" Fifty percent wanted a tougher line.[12] The majority of Americans took Iran's nuclear weapons program as a given because the Bush Administration and the media echo chamber presented it as a given. The only question was what to do about it.

Ahmadinejad at Ground Zero

Ahmadinejad riled up the echo chamber in September 2007 when he asked to visit Ground Zero during a trip to a U.N. conference of world leaders. When word of his request leaked out, according to *Time* magazine, "New York's tabloids hyperventilated."

The *Daily News* opened its report on Ahmadinejad's proposed visit with the line, "Don't even think about it," and shrieked, "If you even think of setting foot near Ground Zero, you can GO TO HELL!"[13] The New York tabloid described Ahmadinejad as a "madman," "an enemy of the U.S. in particular and of civilization in general," and "an accused terrorist, Holocaust denier and proud member of the Axis of Evil."

The *Daily News* then complained, "Just the thought of Ahmadinejad standing on the same ground where the twin towers were destroyed and nearly 3,000 people were killed by terrorists sickened many victims' relatives, White House aides and prominent politicians."

The *Daily News* quoted Jack Lynch, father of a firefighter killed on 9/11: "He's certainly an enemy of ours. He's a nut. How can anyone deny the Holocaust? His presence is not welcome.'" The *Daily News* also revived the debunked "claims by several Americans that he was among the extremists who took them hostage during the 1979 Islamic revolution."[14]

Not to be outdone by its rival tabloid, the *New York Post* opened its report: "No way in hell." The *Post* noted that Ahmadinejad described the Holocaust as "a myth" and quoted Dennis McKeon of a 9/11 support group, "One would think that this was a joke with all of Iran's ties to terrorism and the funding of terrorist attacks."[15]

Almost all the 2008 Presidential candidates tried to score cheap political points by echoing the Ahmadinejad bashing. Mitt Romney suggested, "Ahmadinejad's shockingly audacious request should be met with a vehement no." Romney called Ahmadinejad "a state sponsor of terror," and proposed, "Instead of entertaining Ahmadinejad, we should be indicting him."

Hillary Clinton complained, "It is unacceptable for Iranian President Ahmadinejad, who refuses to renounce and end his own country's support of terrorism, to visit the site of the deadliest terrorist attack on American soil in our nation's history."

Rudy Giuliani fumed, "This is a man who has made threats against America and Israel, is harboring bin Laden's son and other Al Qaeda leaders, is shipping arms to Iraqi insurgents, and is pursuing the development of nuclear weapons. Assisting Ahmadinejad in touring Ground Zero—hallowed ground for all Americans—is outrageous."[16]

Senator Chris Dodd pronounced it "a disgrace and an insult for Mahmoud Ahmadinejad, a man who has given both financial and material support to international terrorist organizations, and who offers rhetoric that spreads only hatred, to be anywhere near Ground Zero."

Lost in all the insults and posturing was a reasonable question: Why not let Ahmadinejad pay his respects at Ground Zero? Why not let him send a message to the Muslim world that 9/11 was an atrocity that everyone, including fundamentalist Muslims, should mourn? Needless to say, no such challenges to the anti-Ahmadinejad fervor got any play in the echo chamber.

Ahmadinejad at Columbia

A couple of weeks after the Iranian president made his Ground Zero request, the anti-Ahmadinejad hysteria flared up again when Columbia University President Lee Bollinger invited him to the Morningside Heights campus. Bollinger's invitation upheld the traditional role of universities to provide forums for the free exchange of opinions and ideas. It was a brave gesture in the midst of the anti-Ahmadinejad media frenzy and pseudo-patriotic chest-pounding. Bollinger seemed to be up to the challenge of defying the echo chamber and offering his university the opportunity to hear another point of view. In announcing the event he said, "It should never be thought that merely to listen to ideas we deplore in any way implies our endorsement of those ideas." While a genuinely free exchange of opinions may be the point of a university education and the hope of a free society, the Ivy League president would soon learn that freedom of speech is not sacred in the echo chamber.

Fox News' Bill O'Reilly led the charge against Columbia, "The University of Havana North." He called the invitation "revolting" and said Bollinger was "hypocritical beyond belief."

A *Daily News* article titled "Columbia University Ripped for Inviting Iranian Thug" cited a long lineup of politicians, religious leaders, and alumni who condemned Bollinger for allowing an "accused terrorist and Holocaust denier to spew his hate on campus." The *Daily News* quoted Abe Foxman of the Anti-Defamation League, "[The event is] a perversion of the concept of freedom of speech." The *Daily News* repeated that Ahmadinejad said Israel should be "wiped off the map," that he called the Holocaust a "myth," and that "the White House and U.S. military leaders have accused Iran of supplying training and weapons to terrorists who are attacking U.S. troops in Iraq."

Presidential candidate John McCain also appeared in the *Daily News* coverage saying, "Rather than rolling out the red carpet for the leader of a terrorist-sponsoring regime, Columbia should be welcoming the Reserve Officers' Training Corps back on campus."

And the *Daily News* noted how presidential candidate Mitt Romney found it disappointing "when our academic institutions can't draw a line between people who bring legitimate differences in perspective versus those who are completely out of touch with reality."[17]

Liberals were stuck trying to figure out how to defend free speech and the mission of the university and also attack Bollinger. City Council Speaker Christine Quinn came up with an interesting formulation. Universities, she conceded, should be "laboratories for a healthy exchange of differing ideas," but such exchanges "should not include state-sponsored terrorism and hate speech." Quinn demanded Bollinger cancel the event and flippantly added, "He can say whatever he wants on any street corner."[18]

Lee Bollinger and the Death of Liberalism

Having boldly taken the national stage, Lee Bollinger had an opportunity to stand up in the face of the nation's media and most powerful politicians and make a statement about the need for a rational dialogue with Ahmadinejad and the Iranian government. Bollinger could have demonstrated an approach to Iran that did not involve threats and insults. But he wilted under the pressure. Instead of engaging in a challenging dialogue as he promised, Bollinger tried to bully the Iranian president.

In introducing Ahmadinejad, the Columbia president barraged his guest with insults. "You exhibit all the signs of a petty and cruel dictator." He arrogantly called Ahmadinejad "quite simply, ridiculous. You are either brazenly provocative or astonishingly uneducated." Bollinger then concluded, "Frankly, and in all candor, Mr. President, I doubt that you will have the intellectual courage to answer these questions.... I do expect you to exhibit the fanatical mindset that characterizes so much of what you say and do.... Today I feel all the weight of the modern civilized world yearning to express the revulsion at what you stand for. I only wish I could do better." Far from embarrassing Ahmadinejad, Bollinger embarrassed himself.

To the uproarious applause of assembled faculty and students, Ahmadinejad slammed Bollinger's rude introduction. "In Iran, tradition requires that when we demand a person to invite to be a speaker, we actually respect our students and the professors by allowing them to make their own judgment, and we don't think it's necessary before this speech is even given to come in with a series of claims and to attempt in a so-called manner to provide vaccination of some sort to our students and our faculty."

Ahmadinejad then schooled Bollinger on free speech at the university, "I think the text read by the dear gentleman here, more than addressing me, was an insult to information and the knowledge of the audience here, present here. In a university environment we must allow people to speak their mind, to allow everyone to talk so that the truth is eventually revealed by all.... We'll just leave that to add up with the claims of respect for freedom and the freedom of speech that's given to us in this country."

The Iranian president then shrewdly noted that Bollinger was mimicking the American media. "Of course, I think that he was affected by the press, the media, and the political, sort of, mainstream line that you read here that goes against the very grain of the need for peace and stability in the world around us."

Ahmadinejad made a great point. In America today, even a liberal Ivy League president safely ensconced in the ivory tower can't resist the power of the echo chamber.

On the night of Bollinger's speech, the media's storyline was put on graphic display. During a Fox News interview with Newt Gingrich, the screenshot abruptly moved away from the image of Gingrich and the interviewer to display a simple question: "Is war the only way to stop Mahmoud?"[19]

Kyle-Lieberman Amendment

Two days after Bollinger's speech, the Senate adopted the Kyle-Lieberman resolution calling on the State Department to designate the Iranian Revolutionary Guard Corps (IRG) a terrorist organization. The measure was adopted in an overwhelming seventy-six to twenty-two vote. Hillary Clinton voted for it. Although Barack Obama later claimed he was opposed, he did not have the courage to show up for the vote. By labeling the IRG a terrorist organization, the Democratic-controlled Congress pulled the plug on negotiations with a large and powerful segment of the Iranian government. The IRG is a 125,000-person organization with ties to every power base in Iran. The IRG is also admired by most Iranians for its heroic stand against Saddam Hussein's invasion during the Iran-Iraq War. Mohammad Khatami, the former reformist president of Iran, warned the United States *not* to label the IRG a terrorist organization, because doing so would preclude any diplomatic settlement. But the echo chamber had been pushing a belligerent approach to Iran since the 2003 "Axis of Evil" speech. Negotiations and compromise were not part of the storyline. And now with the "terrorist" designation, the Democrat-controlled Congress gave George Bush legal sanction to spread the War on Terror to Iran.

Forget it, We Were Wrong...Again

By October 2007, everything was pointing to war with Iran. Administration war hawks led by Dick Cheney just needed a Gulf of Tonkin type of incident to justify the attack they had been planning for years. Defense Secretary Robert Gates, who opposed such an preemptive attack, countered by ordering military commanders in the Persian Gulf to be on guard for any incident that might "accidentally" trigger a military brush-up with Iran.[20] (Gates' order probably had a huge influence on the restraint that U.S. warships displayed when Iranian boats made threatening approaches in a bizarre January 2008 confrontation that eerily resembled the Gulf of Tonkin incident.)

By the winter of 2007, Cheney and the war hawks lost their window of opportunity. A year earlier America's sixteen intelligence agencies compiled a National Intelligence Estimate (NIE) that found the Iranians shut down their nuclear weapons program in 2003. The Administration held back the report for a whole year and tried to force the intelligence community to remove any claims that Iran suspended its nuclear program.[21] Meanwhile Cheney and Bush continued to talk about "the Iranian nuclear weapons program" as if they were certain it presented a grave danger of starting, in Bush's words, "World War III." However, by December 2007, the Administration feared that if it continued to conceal the NIE, the report would soon be leaked to the national media, creating a scandal even more damaging than the leak of the Pentagon Papers by Daniel Ellsberg and Mike Gravel.

On December 3, 2007, the Director of National Intelligence released the NIE. Dick Cheney admitted that the White House had been forced to publicly release the report, "There was a general belief that we all shared that it was important to put out—that it was not likely to stay classified for long, anyway." Asked if the NIE would have been leaked to the media, Cheney responded, "Everything leaks." According to the sources, senior officials in the U.S. intelligence community had made it clear that there were people willing to go to jail in order to reveal the NIE findings and avert an unnecessary war with Iran.[22]

At the close of 2007, the United States stepped away from the brink of another unnecessary war—not because of the media, the Democratic presidential hopefuls, or a Democrat-controlled Congress. America avoided another war because brave intelligence agents were willing to risk their careers and their freedom to avoid another tragedy that might have destroyed tens of thousands of American lives.

CHAPTER FIVE

THE "LIKEABILITY" ELECTION

"You're likeable enough, Hillary. No doubt about it."
Barack Obama to Hillary Clinton
2008 New Hampshire Democratic Debate

"Leading Candidates"

The media echo chamber not only jeopardizes our security by hyping phony threats, it also strangles our democracy by hyping favorite candidates. The media has come to play a bigger role in choosing the president than the political parties or even America's voters. Before most Americans start paying attention to the presidential race, the echo chamber has already promoted certain candidates over others and given them tremendous advantages that prove extremely difficult for other candidates to overcome.

In the early part of the presidential race, today's candidates focus more on garnering favorable media exposure than on winning over voters. With exposure comes fundraising because campaign contributors want to support a potential winner. The media then reports the money raised by candidates as a sign of how well their campaigns are doing and rewards the top money-getters with the labels "frontrunner," "top contender," or "top tier candidate." Even before the vast majority of voters start paying attention to the race, the media has pronounced the "leading candidates." With such media validation, candidates can collect more money which generates even more media coverage.

News coverage also means better name recognition, which is critical at the start of the race when Americans are unfamiliar with most of the candidates. Pollsters call potential voters to ask which candidate they support from a list of names. Respondents will only choose candidates whose names they recognize. As a result, the candidate with the most media exposure gets the highest poll numbers. High poll numbers bring in even more money and generate more media coverage. While the leading candidates ride the succeeding waves of media coverage, fundraising, and polls, the rest of the field struggles to keep afloat.

John McCain

The echo chamber not only builds up candidates by lavishing attention to their fundraising success, it can also destroy important contenders by focusing on their lack of money. In the summer of 2007, John McCain revealed that his fundraising was lower than expected, and his campaign had to lay-off staff members. Immediately, the echo chamber speculated that McCain would drop out, and of course his poll numbers plummeted. However, McCain resisted the pressure and five months later he won the New Hampshire primary. Suddenly the echo chamber, which months before had pronounced McCain DOA, began calling him the candidate to beat.

Journalists respond to criticisms of how they choose the "top candidates" by saying they get their information from pollsters, party insiders, and experts, but the opinions of all those people are based on what they see in the media. Furthermore, journalists can always find someone to give them a quote supporting whatever storyline they are pushing.

The New Cult of Personality

America's fascination with celebrities has had a huge impact on political reporting. Today's news organizations know that running stories on tax reform or Medicare will bore readers and viewers. Since they are just as determined to increase their profits as any other business, their political reporting focuses on two things that interest consumers: personality and celebrity. Stories about candidates tend to focus on their personal narratives or styles rather than experience or positions. Candidates know this and pay media consultants millions of dollars to help them develop an appealing style. Journalists justify this focus on personality by claiming voters are swayed by the candidates' "ability to connect" or their "likeability." But voters are swayed by these superficial qualities in large part because they are presented as more important than the issues. It's also much easier on viewers to choose a candidate based on looks and personality rather than actually pondering the issues. Thus, the echo chamber transforms a presidential race into an *American Idol* contest because that's what the viewers want.

The media and the public are mutually responsible for maintaining the new cult of personality. Polls consistently find that most people are unsatisfied with the quality of American news coverage. A 2000 poll found that sixty-two percent agreed with the statement "political campaigns today seem more like theater or entertainment than like something to be taken seriously."[1] But that's what the consumers want, and in a journalism world dominated by profit-minded media conglomerates, ratings come before all considerations including journalistic integrity. Everyone collaborates with keeping the public in an infantile state. People don't want to be challenged, and the media keeps giving the people what they want—bread and circuses, just like the last days of the Roman Empire.

Time Magazine

To see how much political news has morphed into celebrity news, look at *Time* magazine. *Time* has long been one of the most powerful publications in America. Even though its influence has declined in the past twenty years, the magazine's cover is still a huge prize for any presidential contender. Although most Americans may not buy the issue, millions see it on newsstands. Political news shows also take their cue from *Time* and devote attention to the candidate throughout the week. Of course, the widespread TV exposure generates more name recognition and more campaign contributions.

More than a year away from the primaries, *Time* put Barack Obama on the cover of an October 2006 issue along with the headline "Why Barack Obama Could Be The Next President." Obama got another *Time* cover a year later along with a puff-piece interview. Hillary Clinton snagged two *Time* covers and Mitt Romney got one. Why didn't *Time* deem any other presidential candidates worthy of a cover before the primaries? No one else had a sexy story. Obama, Clinton, and Romney would be firsts: the first African-American, woman, or Mormon president. Of course, that is exciting and historic.

Breaking the white, mostly protestant, male stranglehold on the presidency would be a remarkable advance for equality in America. But the echo chamber's focus on certain personalities and life stories over qualifications and issues transforms the presidential race into a contest over what the media calls "likeability."

The Likeability Factor

Self-help guru Tim Sanders popularized the word "likeability" in a 2005 book, *The Likeability Factor.* Here are Sanders' measures of likeability:

1. Smile often
2. Pleasant tone of voice
3. Positive, optimistic attitude
4. Approachable
5. Good listener
6. Build other people's self-confidence and make them feel good about themselves; very helpful

7. Skilled at being sensitive
8. Understanding of other people's thoughts, feelings, and experiences
9. Connect with others' interests such as hobbies, hometowns, and affiliations

This sounds more like Oprah Winfrey or a really good kindergarten teacher, not a Commander in Chief. But the media seized on "likeability" as a key factor in the presidential race because it justifies their hyper-focus on personality. The leading candidates also try to conform to the likeability formula by avoiding strong positions that might challenge voters. They want voters to believe that they understand everyone's thoughts, feelings, and experiences; that everyone is special and everyone's opinion is valid. No wonder our national political discussion is so vapid. The talking heads reinforce this absence of real issues in the national debate by focusing on who is most "likeable."

Barack Obama is a perfect example. He's a very interesting guy behind closed doors, but he never shows it on the campaign trail. A typical Obama speech avoids anything that might alienate anyone and offers lots of happy talk about "hope" and "change." This is not entirely Obama's fault. He knows strong positions will antagonize some people and make him less "likeable." He knows people tend to focus on style over words, and an effective speech today makes people "feel" good about themselves rather than challenges them to think for themselves. Obama has everything he needs to be a successful politician today: likeability and charisma. Why would he want to spoil that advantage by actually discussing the issues in depth or displaying some genuine but potentially "unlikeable" personality traits?

Obama got burned the one time he broke out of his likeable persona. Ironically, it happened when the "likeability issue" was raised during a presidential debate days before the New Hampshire primary. Hillary Clinton was asked what she would "say to the voters of New Hampshire…who see a resume and like it but are hesitating on the likeability issue, where they seem to like Barack Obama more."

Clinton gave a very likeable response, "Well, that hurts my feelings (laughter)…but I'll try to go on (laughter). He's very likeable. I agree with that. I don't think I'm that bad."

In a moment of uncharacteristic candor, Obama disdainfully chimed in, "You're likeable enough, Hillary," making his true feelings quite plain. After Obama lost the New Hampshire vote, the echo chamber cited this moment when Obama showed his disdain for Hillary as a turning point. It seems voters did not like Obama's "unlikeable" flash of genuine feeling. Such touchy-feely considerations might be relevant if we were electing America's Next Top Model but have no place in choosing the next Commander in Chief.

Barack's No-Show Votes

Barack Obama is also a great example of how the echo chamber becomes invested in the storyline it created for a candidate and refuses to report anything that deviates from it. By far the most compelling and politically talented politician on the current American political scene, Obama also has a great back-story— growing up the son of biracial couple and becoming an extremely successful adult without much support from his father. Everyone should admire his meteoric rise to the apex of American politics along with his brave stand against the Iraq War in the face of warmongering from both parties and the national media.

However, Obama has flaws the media conveniently under-reported during their build-up of his candidacy for president. While a state senator, he refused to vote on the issue of abortion when it came up five times. He refused to stand up for "the right to choose" which he publicly supports and instead voted "present," essentially a non-vote. Why didn't he vote according to his vaunted principles? It was politically expedient not to register a vote on abortion.

Obama also ducked a recent Senate vote to label the Iranian Revolutionary Guard as a "terrorist organization" and basically give George Bush a green light to start a war with Iran. While all the other senators running for president voted on the resolution, Obama was a no-show. Shouldn't Obama's refusal to take a stand on politically tough votes have sparked widespread debate in the media about his commitment to principle over politics? Isn't this an important question for voters trying to decide whether he will make a good president? The media willfully ignored these crucial questions which deviated from their preferred storyline.

Obamagate

Obama also had a financial scandal the national press largely ignored. In November 2006, the *Chicago Tribune* reported that Obama purchased a $1.65 million Georgian revival home on Chicago's South Side in 2005 at $300,000 less than the asking price. On the very same day, Antoin "Tony" Rezko, an Obama fundraiser and slum lord, bought an empty lot adjacent to Obama's new home at the asking price from the same owner. Rezko then sold a 1,500-square-foot slice of it to Obama for $104,000, a fair sum in that market. Rezko was later indicted for extortion and influence peddling in the Illinois state legislature.

Did Rezko orchestrate his same-day purchase of the lot at full price so that the seller would give Obama a break on the adjacent house? Did Rezko do this so he could call in a favor from the rising Illinois political star? Obama simply denied any arrangement with Rezko claiming that he got such a good deal because the house was being unloaded in a "fire sale."[2] One might wonder why the seller sold to Obama at the fire-sale price but Rezko at the market rate. But Obama's fire-sale explanation was sufficient for the national media. Whatever discussion it did generate was quickly drowned out in the echo chamber because the media did not want anything to complicate the feel-good story of the charismatic, resilient up-and-comer.

Obama is not corrupt, but his judgment in this instance can be questioned. By refusing to ask legitimate questions, the media never forced Obama to fully explain his thinking to the American public.

"The Biggest Fairy Tale I've Ever Seen"
On the day before the 2008 New Hampshire primary, Bill Clinton voiced his frustration with the media for

giving Obama a free ride. The former president was upset that the media echoed Obama's claim to be the anti-war candidate even though he repeatedly voted to fund the war. Clinton fumed about the media "trumpeting [Obama's] superior judgment and how he had been against the war every year." "Give me a break," Clinton added. "This whole thing is the biggest fairy tale I've ever seen."[3] Clinton was right. Obama may have opposed the war initially, but he consistently voted to fund the war until a majority of Democratic voters began to oppose funding—hardly a profile in courage. The media gave him a free pass for those votes, among others.

Although the media covered Bill Clinton's outburst and gave particular attention to his "fairy tale" line, another line in his speech was much more interesting: "Just because of the sanitizing coverage that's in the media doesn't mean the facts aren't out there." Clinton did not elaborate on those "facts."

But during the debate before the South Carolina primary, Hillary brought up Obama's present votes on abortion and his legal work representing his "contributor Rezko in his slum landlord business in inner-city Chicago." The *Chicago Tribune* noted that prior to that moment only the Chicago newspapers gave the Rezko story any play.[4] Fortunately for

Obama, most of the national media continued to ignore the story much to Hillary's chagrin.

The problem with the media turning a blind eye to certain stories that might impede the rise of a favored candidate is that when those stories eventually come out—and they always do—they might be even more damaging than if they were dealt with at the start of the campaign. In Obama's case, old stories involving Rezko and his inflammatory pastor Jeremiah Wright suddenly burst into the "news" late in the primary contest. The resulting media frenzies presented serious obstacles to Obama's ability to sew up the nomination in the spring of 2008 and further divided the Democratic Party.

"This Guy Just Said 'Cocaine' Again!"

The story of Obama's cocaine use is a good example of how a candidate can be hurt when rivals revive an under-reported story at a crucial moment in a campaign. Obama was smart to "get out in front of the story" and expose his past drug use before the media did. By revealing it in his 2004 autobiography, *Dreams from My Father: A Story of Race and Inheritance*, Obama was able to avoid scandal by weaving his drug use into a narrative of how he overcame a difficult past. With the notable exception of Fox News, the media repeated that positive spin in the little coverage it got.

The story remained dormant throughout the campaign until a month before the Iowa caucus when the Clinton campaign sent an email to supporters and reporters: "It's important for Democrats to understand the strengths and weaknesses of each candidate. Clinton's negatives are well known, Obama's less so. Any shortcomings, inconsistencies, or misstatements in Obama's past will be exploited by Republicans in the fall campaign if he's the nominee. It's best for Democrats to vet them now."[5] Actually, it was best for Clinton to "vet them" in the weeks leading up to Iowa.

A day after that email went out, William Shaheen, co-chairman of Mrs. Clinton's national and New Hampshire campaigns, raised Obama's drug use in an interview with the *Washington Post* suggesting that voters should study Obama's background before they vote for him and warning that Republicans would surely exploit the issue in a general election contest. "It'll be, 'When was the last time? Did you ever give drugs to anyone? Did you sell them to anyone?'" Shaheen said. "There are so many openings for Republican dirty tricks. It's hard to overcome."[6] After reports of Shaheen's comments rattled around the echo chamber, Clinton asked for his resignation and he publicly apologized, which kept the story in the headlines for another day.

Days later, Clinton's top adviser, Mark Penn, appeared on MSNBC with Obama's top adviser, David Axelrod, and John Edwards's strategist, Joe Trippi, to discuss Shaheen's comments. Penn did his best to "distance" himself from Shaheen's scandal mongering while simultaneously keeping it alive by dropping the word *cocaine,* saying that the Clinton campaign had not raised the "cocaine use." Penn's brazenness appalled even the seasoned politico Trippi who couldn't contain his disgust, "This guy just said 'cocaine' again!"

Weeks later, after the Shaheen brouhaha was dying down, another Clinton supporter Robert Johnson, the founder of the Black Entertainment Television network, brought up Obama's drug use and generated more headlines. Days later, he duly apologized.

The Likeable Huckabee?

No candidate has benefited more from the echo chamber's fixation on likeability than Mike Huckabee. Journalists love his personal story of losing 100 pounds and his supposedly great sense of humor. *Newsweek* claimed, "It's hard not to like Mike Huckabee," and *The Nation* said he has "real charm." Conan O'Brien, Bill Maher and Jay Leno invited him on their shows to yuck it up.

Everyone in the echo chamber fell in love with Huckabee. Why? He believes only Christians get to go to heaven. "If you're with Jesus Christ, we know how it turns out in the final moment. I've read the last chapter in the book, and we do end up winning." One of his first acts as governor of Arkansas was to block Medicaid from funding an abortion for a mentally retarded teenager who had been raped by her stepfather.

He not only supports a constitutional amendment banning abortion, he also favors religion over science. "Science changes with every generation and with new discoveries and God doesn't. So I'll stick with God if the two are in conflict." He even questions evolution. "If anybody wants to believe that they are the descendants of a primate, they are certainly welcome to do it." He refused to back away from his statement that AIDS victims should be quarantined, and he supports flying the Confederate flag over the South Carolina state capitol. This is a media darling?

Huckabee has also engaged in borderline-corrupt schemes that make Obama's real estate deal with Rezko look like the height of propriety. Huckabee paid himself as a consultant to his own senatorial campaign and set up a "wedding registry" at Target and Dillard's department store so the people of Arkansas could buy his wife and him gifts when the Huckabees renewed their marriage vows. If Huckabee fans didn't want to buy him a Kitchen Aid mixer or a Jack La Lanne power juicer, the governor arranged for the registry to accept cash. "Message from the couple," the registry noted, "Target GiftCards are welcome."[7] Aside from Matt Taibbi of *Rolling Stone,* the media embraced the "likeable" Huckabee and overlooked facts that would interfere with the love fest.

The "Inevitable" Hillary Clinton

While the echo chamber pronounced Obama and Huckabee "likeable," Hillary Clinton was called "inevitable." Her big lead in the polls during the summer of 2007 seemed to support the media's storyline about Hillary's coronation march to the Democratic nomination. The gullible media, however, put too much trust in the polls which favored Clinton because of her unparalleled name recognition. Once Democrats started paying attention to the race in the fall of 2007, Clinton's poll numbers dropped.

Democrats began to see that Clinton was closer to George Bush on the issues than they thought. Hillary voted for the Patriot Act and then supported its renewal in 2006, despite revelations that the government was using it to infringe on the very liberties that our founders held sacred. She is a hawk and a consistent supporter of Bush's belligerence toward Iraq and Iran. She even voted for the war in Iraq without bothering to read the ninety-page National Intelligence Estimate, which showed that the Administration's case for war was weaker than the media was reporting. She then repeatedly authorized billions for the Pentagon to enrich Halliburton in no-bid contracts. When ousting Saddam brought chaos to the streets of Iraq and death to thousands of innocents, she blamed the Iraqis, "The American military has succeeded. It is the Iraqi government which has failed to make the tough decisions that are important for their own people."[8]

A candidate so out of touch with typical Democratic voters could only be labeled "inevitable" by a gullible, out of touch media.

John Edwards' Hair Cut Scandal

While the media gives favored candidates free passes for their misdeeds, it has no problem trashing candidates for absolutely nothing. A perfect example of this is the media frenzy over John Edwards' haircuts. The blog *Politico* broke the big news on April 16, 2007, that John Edwards "spent $400 on February 20th and another $400 on March 7th at a top Beverly Hills men's stylist, Torrenueva Hair Designs."

Matt Drudge picked up the story and a day later the *Los Angeles Times* ran a report, "Two $400 stylings may cost John Edwards' campaign in shear mockery."

The AP later joined the sniggering with an article titled "Edwards' Haircuts Cost a Pretty Penny," which opened with a cheap shot, "Looking pretty is costing John Edwards' presidential campaign a lot of pennies." The repeated use of the word "pretty" was a riff on a popular YouTube video of Edwards caught on camera while waiting for a television interview. Edwards primps his hair up and checks himself out in a mirror to the tune of the song *I'm So Pretty*. According to the AP, "FEC records show Edwards also availed himself of $250 in services from a trendy salon and spa in Dubuque, Iowa, and $225 in services from the Pink Sapphire in Manchester, N.H., which is described on its website as 'a unique boutique for the mind, body, and face' that caters mostly to women."

Edwards' "day at the spa" fit the media's running storyline: A vain man who pretends to care for the poor but is really only concerned with his grooming. The AP story, however, buried certain facts until the end of the article, "Pink Sapphire co-owner Ariana Franggos said the two payments last month—$150 on March 7th and $75 on March 20th—were for doing Edwards' makeup for television appearances."

The owner also assured the AP, "This poor guy. I'm telling you, I promise he's not in here getting facials and cucumber peels on his eyes or anything," she said. In other words, Edwards, like all politicians, was just getting makeup for a TV appearance, but the AP buried that fact at the end of the article.

So why would the AP even mention that the Pink Sapphire "mainly caters to women"? Why did the media push such trumped up stories about Edwards despite the facts? Even before the haircut story appeared, the media had embraced a caricature of Edwards as a vain, primping "Breck Boy." This was the notion behind conservative Rush Limbaugh asking whether Edwards might be our "first female president" or *New York Times* liberal Maureen Dowd labeling Edwards the "metrosexual-in-chief." While the echo chamber excoriated Anne Coulter for calling Edwards a faggot, they happily played upon the sentiment behind the slur when they harped on Edwards' $400 haircuts.[9] The Edwards campaign never recovered.

Edwards' Mistake

John Edwards has all the makings of a strong candidate. Like the successful Democratic presidential candidates of the past forty years, he is a white southerner who could easily contest southern states in a general election. Even before the haircut scandal, Edwards doomed himself with the media by centering his campaign on poverty, an unglamorous issue that the media has ignored assiduously for thirty years! When was the last time anyone on *Meet the Press* even mentioned the word *poverty*?

Edwards' incisive assessment of two Americas— one rich and one poor—was not just an indictment of the rich or an indifferent government. He was also challenging a media that pretends the poor don't exist in America. If the media took Edwards' message seriously, they would suddenly have to start covering un-sexy stories about the ghetto or rural poverty the way they did back in the 1970s. Political talk shows like *Hardball* would have to hold discussions about impoverished children—a real ratings killer to be sure. Rather than take Edwards' message seriously, it was much easier for the echo chamber to focus on his style and personality and dismiss him as a vain, hypocritical pretty boy.

Obama, the New Bobby Kennedy

By January 2008, the same two candidates that the media celebrated and protected from the very beginning of the race were leading in the polls. After Obama won a surprising victory in Iowa, the echo chamber began pronouncing *him* the "inevitable" nominee and jumping off the Clinton bandwagon in droves. Suddenly, not only had Hillary lost her sparkle but Bill Clinton had, too. The *New York Times* described a "sluggish" Bill Clinton speaking to "listless," "smallish," and "sleepy crowds" in New Hampshire. "Is this what it would have been like had Elvis been reduced to playing Reno?"[10] In the days leading up to the New Hampshire vote, almost all the talking heads in the media parroted the same storyline: Obama was the new Bobby Kennedy and his victory marked the "End of the Clinton Era."

Hillary's "Edmund Muskie Moment"

Our celebrity-obsessed media loves a gaffe, especially one that reflects the echo chamber's storyline. After Clinton's loss in the Iowa primary, the media was primed for a Hillary breakdown akin to Howard Dean's scream in 2004 or Edmund Muskie's tearing up in 1972 after a New Hampshire newspaper attacked his wife. In each case the media transformed an insignificant moment into a major "news" story that had a significant impact on the presidential race.

The media got its "meltdown" when Hillary became misty during a coffee klatch with fifteen women in New Hampshire. Someone asked Clinton how she held up on the campaign trail. "It's not easy, it's not easy," Clinton said shaking her head, her eyes becoming a bit watery. "I couldn't do it if I didn't passionately believe it was the right thing to do. This is very personal for me."

The media went wild reporting about Hillary "crying." The fact that she didn't shed a single tear but merely welled-up didn't matter. The media was not about to allow the fact to get in the way of a good story. MSNBC, Fox News, and CNN all discussed "Hillary's Edmund Muskie Moment." Fox's conservative commentators Michelle Malkin and Bill Kristol even suggested the cry was calculated to remind people, in Malkin's words, that "she has a womb" and "that she's not the glacier that people think she is." The media echo chamber played the video over and over and reached a general consensus that, calculated or not, Hillary's cry finished her. After reviewing the media coverage, Comedy Central's Jon Stewart joked, "That's it? That's the emotional breakdown that blows the election for her? I'm glad no one here ever sees me get a flu shot."

While every political commentator assessed the impact of the image of Hillary's "cry," no one focused on her words, which also played incessantly during the media frenzy. "Some of us are right, and some of us are wrong. Some of us are ready, and some of us are not. Some of us know what we will do on day one, and some of us haven't really thought that through enough. And so when we look at the array of problems we have and the potential for it, getting really…spinning out of control. This is one of the most important elections America's ever faced." Hillary had been making this point about Obama's inexperience for months with no effect. Now the echo chamber made sure that everyone heard Clinton stoke fears that Obama would not be ready for the job—over and over again.

In the days leading up to the New Hampshire vote, the echo chamber also repeatedly played another video—Iranian boats reportedly threatening U.S. naval forces in the Strait of Hormuz. That video combined with reports of the plummeting stock market added poignancy to Hillary's teary shot at Obama.

Five days after Clinton lost to Obama among Iowa women by five percentage points, Clinton beat Obama among New Hampshire women by twelve points.[11] Clearly Hillary wound up winning the New Hampshire primary because women sympathized with her and resented the media's hounding her for "crying." Clinton's warning that Obama isn't "ready" constantly replayed by the media also moved late-deciding voters. In Iowa just eighteen percent of late-deciding women voted for Clinton compared with thirty-two percent for Obama and thirty-one percent for Edwards. New Hampshire women who made up their minds in the three days before Election Day favored Clinton by forty-four percent to thirty-two percent.[12]

If the media treated Clinton's misty moment like the insignificant incident that it was rather than constantly replaying and analyzing it, Obama probably would have maintained some of his ten point lead and won his second primary. In a strange way, the echo chamber's hyping of Clinton's emotional and political downfall wound up saving her campaign.

CHAPTER SIX

MAVERICK IN
THE ECHO CHAMBER

*GRAVEL: Who the hell are we going to nuke? Tell me,
Barack. Barack, who do you want to nuke?*

*OBAMA: I'm not planning to nuke anybody right now,
Mike, I promise.*

First Democratic Presidential Debate,
South Carolina 2007

Mike Gravel's first lesson in how the media manipulates our democracy came in 1968 when he was thirty-eight and running for the U.S. Senate. A week before the election, the *Anchorage News,* the most influential newspaper in Alaska, his home state, ran a scathing article under the byline of one of its reporters. It later came out that the article was surreptitiously written by his opponent's campaign. Drew Pearson, the legendary political columnist, also bashed Gravel in his nationally syndicated column at the behest of Mike's opponent.

Forty years later, Gravel knew that running for president was going to be an uphill battle not only against his well-funded opponents but also against the media. But he figured that if the voters could hear his message, he might have a shot.

"The Debates"

Ideally, the debates provide an opportunity for all the presidential candidates to bypass the media and introduce themselves to millions of people. This is especially helpful for the so-called lower tier candidates including Mike Gravel.

NBC's Brian Williams, the host of the first debate, ignored Gravel as if, in the Senator's words, he were a "potted plant." But Gravel made a big impression by refusing to go along with the media's fawning treatment of the top tier candidates: "It's like going into the Senate, you know the first time you get there you're all excited—'My God, how did I ever get here?' And then, about six months later, you say, 'How the hell did the rest of them get here?' (Laughter.) And I got to tell you, after standing up with them, some of these people frighten me! They frighten me!"

Gravel defied the war mongering on Iran's nuclear bomb threat: "When you have mainline candidates that turn around and say that there's nothing off the table with respect to Iran, that's code for using nukes, nuclear devices. I got to tell you. I'm president of the

United States; there will be no preemptive wars with nuclear devices. To my mind, it's immoral, and it's been immoral for the last fifty years as part of American foreign policy." Gravel called out Obama for refusing to rule out using nukes on Iran, "Who the hell are we going to nuke? Tell me, Barack. Barack, who do you want to nuke?"

Obama smiled, "I'm not planning to nuke anybody right now, Mike, I promise."

"Good," Gravel barked, "We're safe then, for a while." Gravel went on to give viewers a history lesson on Iran: "We've sanctioned them for twenty-six years. We've scared the bejesus out of them when the president says they're evil. Well, you know something? These things don't work. They don't work. We need to recognize them. And you know something, who is the greatest violator of the Non-Proliferation Treaty? The United States of America. We signed a pledge that we would begin to disarm, and we're not doing it. We're expanding our nukes. Who the hell are we going to nuke?"

Gravel challenged all the mindless talk about American's enemies, "We have no important enemies. What we need to do is to begin to deal with the rest of the world as equals, and we don't do that. We spend more as a nation on defense than all the rest of the world put together. Who are we afraid of? Who are you afraid of, Brian? I'm not, and Iraq has never been a threat to us. *We* invaded *them*." And he even took on the military-industrial complex by saying it "not only controls our government lock, stock, and barrel, but they control our culture."

The reaction to Mike's performance in that first debate was huge. Contributions flooded the campaign's empty coffers. People were excited to hear someone break the group-speak and defy the media storyline. But that kind of defiance was too much for the mainstream media. By the time the debates started, the media had already chosen their darlings and had begun shutting down the upstarts. After Gravel upset the apple cart in the first debate, CNN announced that it was excluding him from the next debate.

"Potted Plant"

When word got out that CNN had decided to exclude Gravel, his supporters used the power of the Internet to contact each other and flood CNN's offices with emails demanding his participation. CNN eventually caved but did its best to marginalize Gravel during the debate by physically positioning him on the far left of the stage, outside of the TV camera's wide shot of the candidates.

CNN also limited Gravel's questions and the time he was allowed to respond. Below are the candidates as they ranked in the national polls at the time of the CNN debate along with the time they were allowed to speak and the number of questions they were asked:

Clinton	14:26	15 questions
Obama	16:00	16 questions
Edwards	11:42	13 questions
Richardson	10:48	11 questions
Dodd	8:28	9 questions
Biden	7:58	10 questions
Kucinich	9:02	9 questions
Gravel	5:37	10 questions

Notice how the amount of time given to the candidates matched up almost perfectly with their poll rankings. (Obama, who was second in polling, got about ninety seconds more time than the front-running Clinton.) The other debates followed this pattern of weighting the speaking times heavily in favor of the front-runners.

Here again the media chokes democracy. By limiting the ability of the so-called lower tier candidates to communicate their positions and draw contrasts with the media darlings, the debate hosts limit the discussion and reinforce the perception that there are only a few serious contenders. One might expect the Democratic Party to jump in and insist that all candidates receive equal time. DNC chairman Howard Dean, a onetime lower tier candidate, could have stood up against the inequitable allotment of air time. But whatever commitment to grassroots democracy Dean had as a candidate disappeared when he took over the DNC. Dean and the DNC liked that the media was whittling down the field and featuring just a few candidates. They wanted the contest to be decided quickly with minimal debate that might harm their eventual nominee. Dean certainly wasn't going to buck the networks over a lower tier troublemaker like Mike Gravel.

Tavis Smiley

One exception to the rigged debate formats was a PBS debate hosted by Tavis Smiley at Howard University. Smiley asked each candidate the same question and allowed equal response time to everyone. Not only was PBS's debate the fairest, it also provided its audience with the most wide-ranging discussion. It's no coincidence that the only fair debate was on public television, or that the only fair debate catered to an

African-American audience. No other group of people has a greater interest in challenging the consensus. Neither party has served the African-American community well over the recent decades. The Republicans still retain a powerful racist wing and the Democrats take the black vote for granted.

Smiley and the PBS debate organizers wanted to hear something different than the usual pabulum, and Gravel gave them something different, "You have heard these nostrums before. You've heard it ten years ago, you've heard twenty years ago—why doesn't it change? The Democratic Party hasn't done appreciably better than the Republican Party in solving these problems. It has to be solved by the people, not by your leaders." As Gravel spoke, applause erupted from the audience while the camera caught Al Sharpton nodding his head in agreement. Not everyone, however, appreciated Mike attacking his own party's failures.

George Stephanopoulos: Skunk at the Party

After the Tavis Smiley debate, George Stephanopoulos whined, "In every single one of his answers, Mike Gravel was determined to be the *skunk at the party* and attack the other candidates." Stephanopoulos was frustrated that Gravel wasn't playing nice with his fellow Democrats and was actually questioning their positions and the Democratic Party. Stephanopoulos joined the rest of the echo chamber in commending the other Democrats for being so civil and polite to each other and unified against the Bush Administration. He did not like that Mike Gravel was pointing out that the Democrats were also guilty of violating the trust of the American people.

Since the viewing audience for a typical primary debate is less than the average sitcom, post-debate analysts like Stephanopoulos hold a tremendous power over how the rest of the media reports the debate and how the public processes it. During the few times debate commentators even mentioned Gravel's performances, it was always dismissively.

The Gay Debate

It wasn't just the mainstream media that tried to exclude Gravel from the debates. In the summer of 2007, the Human Rights Campaign, a gay rights advocacy group, and LOGO television announced that they were inviting all the presidential candidates of both parties, except Mike, to the first ever gay issues forum.

Gravel had been the most outspoken defender of gay rights and was praised by *The Advocate* for being "unabashedly pro-gay marriage."[1] The top candidates certainly didn't want him around to bash their opposition to marriage equality and accuse them of keeping gays in second-class citizenship. Did the HRC bow to the star power of the top tier? Who knows? Officially the HRC hid behind money, claiming that Gravel failed to meet HRC's $100,000 fundraising threshold. The campaign countered by immediately contacting the gay press and websites which quoted Mike's disgust, "That this kind of censorship should come from the community that I am the greatest advocate [of]. It is not absurd; it's to the edge of stupidity. That they would set up a criteria of not having enough money raised—all political scientists recognize that money is the corruption of the political system."

Gravel continued, "They [HRC] are saying I'm not greedy or corrupt enough to meet the standards set by Hillary and Obama and Edwards. You hear Edwards saying he can't get his arms around [gay marriage]. Is that the garbage HRC want to put before the people?"

All of the major gay publications rose to Mike's defense. *Queerty* wrote, "Gravel may not be the leading Democratic candidate, but HRC's definitely shown their true colors—they're more interested in moderate, wealthy politicians than those willing to rock the boat, as Gravel has done."[2] After being flooded with complaints and being threatened with a massive protest, HRC bowed to the public pressure and invited Mike to the debate.

After reading Mike's open letter thanking the gay community, one supporter responded, "Excellent rethinking on the part of the debate organizers...I really look forward to watching the debate. I probably would have skipped it otherwise since I am so tired of the mainstream Democratic Party's doublespeak and hypocrisy when it comes to gay rights." On the night of the debate, Mike once again challenged the Democrats to embrace full equality for all Americans including marriage equality for gays and lesbians.

Although HRC backed down, it set a bad precedent by trying to establish a fundraising threshold to shut Gravel out of a debate.

"Our Guys Should Talk"

At the end of a NAACP presidential debate in July 2007, John Edwards walked up to Hillary Clinton and whispered in front of an open mic, "At some time in the fall, we should try to have a more serious...smaller group."

Hillary knew exactly what he meant. "We've got to cut the number," she murmured. "I think there was an effort by our campaigns to do that.... It got somehow detoured. We've got to get back to it." Walking away Clinton added, "Our guys should talk." News of the overheard conversation raised little notice in the echo chamber. The media was unbothered that candidates were collaborating to short circuit the democratic process and limit the national political debate because that's exactly what the media wanted. Gravel was spoiling the storyline. In the fall, just as Edwards and Clinton had discussed, the networks kicked Gravel out of the debates.

But not before the "Man from Alaska" got in one last shot.

"Hillary, I'm Ashamed of You"

In the summer of 2007, the Clinton campaign looked unstoppable. Gravel continued to criticize her during the debates and in his frequent blog screeds on the *Huffington Post,* including a popular one titled, "Why Hillary Scares Me." But none of the other candidates dared to aggressively challenge Hillary "the Inevitable." Mike's last shot at Hillary came during a September NBC debate on the same day she joined a majority of her Senate colleagues to support a resolution labeling the Iranian Revolutionary Guard, a terrorist organization. That afternoon Gravel and his communications director discussed the vote and decided to bring it up during that night's debate to draw attention to the fact that Hillary is a war hawk. There would be added drama to the confrontation because Clinton and Gravel were set to stand next to each other that night on the dais. The stage was set for a great video news clip to feed the media.

During the debate, Gravel got to say a grand total of 776 words (the next lowest total was Dennis Kucinich with 1,423 words), but Mike made every word count.

The debate opened with each candidate promising to end the war in Iraq but refusing to guarantee that U.S. troops would be out before the end of their first Administrations in 2013.

Mike cut through all the nonsense and outlined how all the senators running for president could use their senatorial powers to force a withdrawal. Tim Russert was totally befuddled, "Senator, are you suggesting that these candidates suspend their campaigns, go back to Washington, and for forty consecutive days vote on the war?"

Gravel was equally confused, "If it stops the killing, my God, yes, do it!"

Then Mike brought up Hillary and Iran, "And Tim, you're really missing something. This is fantasyland. We are talking about ending the war. My God, we're just starting a war right today! There was a vote in the Senate today. Joe Lieberman, who authored the Iraq resolution, has offered another resolution, and it is essentially a fig leaf to let George Bush go to war with Iran. I want to congratulate Biden for voting against it, Dodd for voting against it. And I am ashamed of you, Hillary, for voting *for* it. You're not going to get another shot at this because what happens if this war ensues, we invade, and they're looking for an excuse to do it. And Obama was not even there to vote."

Russert then turned to Clinton, "Senator Clinton, I want to give you a chance to respond."

And Clinton burst out laughing. "I don't know where to start." The moment was featured on several newscasts that night.

The next day, Mike posted a well-received *Huffington Post* titled "Hillary, War with Iran is No Laughing Matter." Mike wrote, "Hillary, I'm glad to see you got a good laugh when I confronted you during last week's debate over your vote calling the Iranian Revolutionary Guard (IRG) a terrorist organization. The American public finally got to see your cavalier attitude toward our march to war. Your vote, however, is no laughing matter."

A couple of days later, a piece in the *New York Times* about Hillary's "cackle" triggered commentary throughout the echo chamber about whether or not her laugh was sincere. In a media obsessed with style and celebrity, a vote for war with Iran is not nearly as important as an awkward laugh.

NBC

Mike's "Hillary, I'm ashamed of you" moment must have ruffled a lot of feathers because a couple of weeks later, NBC announced that they were excluding him from the next debate on October 30th in Philadelphia.

To minimize the public uproar, NBC waited until 5 p.m. the Friday before the debate to inform Gravel's staff that he was not invited. Although Mike had attended eleven prior debates including two sponsored by NBC, the network suddenly conjured up arbitrary polling and fundraising requirements specifically designed to exclude him. None of the previous debates held such requirements.

When the campaign called NBC directly to find out why Mike was suddenly barred from attending, Chuck Todd, NBC news' political director, said there were three criteria Gravel did not meet: namely that he had not campaigned in New Hampshire and/or Iowa at least fourteen times in the past year, that he was not polling at five percent, and that he hadn't raised a million dollars.

It was abundantly clear that NBC just wanted Gravel out of the debate. Mike had traveled to New

Hampshire and Iowa at least fourteen times, and according to the latest CNN poll, he was tied with Joe Biden, Dennis Kucinich, and Chris Dodd. The only reason NBC excluded Gravel was because he hadn't raised enough money. By stifling Gravel's voice on the basis of fundraising dollars, NBC was reinforcing the power of money over America's democracy.

Saturday Night Live Speaks Out

A few days after the Philadelphia debate, *Saturday Night Live* ran a sketch in which host Brian Williams informs the presidential candidates assembled for the debate that the media are coddling Hillary.

"Gentlemen, I'm going to have to run; I have a fifteen-minute pre-debate interview with Senator Clinton. We're going to ask her about her first 100 days in office," Williams says. "I wish you all good luck tonight, though we, again, in the media have pretty much made up our minds to go with Senator Clinton. We'll see you in a few minutes." Whether NBC dumped Gravel at Clinton's request may never be known, but *SNL* was on to something when it slammed the media for favoring Hillary in the fall of 2007.

But as Hillary soon learned, the press is fickle and today's media darling often becomes tomorrow's goat.

In February 2008, *SNL* aired a skit in which CNN's debate hosts fawn over Obama and ask him questions like "Are you comfortable? Can we get you anything?" During a real debate a few days later, Clinton referenced the *SNL* skit: "Can I just point out that in the last several debates, I seem to get the first question ALL the time…if anybody saw *Saturday Night Live* maybe we should ask Barack if he's comfortable and needs another pillow."

The media doesn't collectively conspire to favor a particular candidate. It just seems to play favorites because once a storyline emerges about a collapsing campaign or an "inevitable" candidate, the media generates stories that comport with the storyline and spikes stories that deviate from it. The media coverage also influences the journalists themselves. Debate hosts become deferential toward the leading candidate and aggressive toward the sputtering contender. The echo chamber consequently pushes a sagging campaign toward collapse while it feeds the momentum of the ascendant candidate.

The "Alternative Debate"

The Gravel campaign did not take the exclusion from the Philadelphia debate lying down. At great expense, the campaign rented an auditorium around the corner from the debate venue and set it up so that Mike and an audience could watch the debate while the Senator used TiVo to stop the video and give his running commentary. Hundreds attended the event and thousands watched the webcast. Without time restrictions, Mike was able to make several important points about the nature of contemporary presidential debates:

▶ *"Where's Mike?"* Isn't it amazing that GE and NBC could suddenly drop me from the debates and none of my opponents would even comment on it? It's like Stalin's Russia when someone would just stop showing up for work, but no one in the office dared to ask, "Hey, whatever happened to Ivan?" What does it say about the state of American politics and the Democratic Party when our presidential candidates don't have the guts to question a TV network?

▶ *Hillary Bashing:* Great to see Edwards and Obama finally challenge Clinton for supporting the march toward war with Iran. For months I have been educating the public about this trumped up crisis with Iran. My "I'm ashamed of you, Hillary" moment got me in big trouble with the power elite including NBC's parent company GE, a major military contractor. But Edwards and Obama's Hillary-bashing rings false. Was it based on genuine disagreement or just political calculation? Obama, after all, refused to even show up for the vote on the Iranian Revolutionary Guard.

▶ *Russert and Iran:* Russert repeatedly pestered each of the candidates: "Will you pledge that when you're president, Iran will not develop nukes?" Was that a question? A twisted mantra? Or was it a demand for a profession of faith that we needed to bomb Iran? Talk about trying to undermine diplomacy. Enough of Tim Russert!

▶ *Carrots and Sticks:* During the debate, all the candidates talked about using "Carrots and Sticks" in dealing with Iran. Carrots and Sticks? Maybe a good way to start diplomacy would be to show the Iranians some respect and stop referring to them as donkeys that must be bribed or beaten into compliance.

▶ *Tim Russert's UFO:* Once again Russert assumed his role as the media establishment's hatchet man. In my last debate, he sandbagged, me asking about my decades old bankruptcies. Why not ask Hillary about the Rose law firm billing records? Or Obama about his suspect real estate deal? This time Russert's victim was Dennis Kucinich.

Russert: "Congressman Kucinich...this is a serious question. The godmother of your daughter, Shirley MacLaine, writes in her new book that you've sighted a UFO over her home in Washington state (laughter), that you found the encounter extremely moving, that it was a triangular craft, silent and hovering, that you felt a connection to your heart, and heard direction in your mind. Now, did you see a UFO? (Laughter.)"

Kucinich: "I did. And the rest of the account (interrupted by laughter), I didn't...I...it was unidentified flying object, okay. It's like, it's unidentified. I saw something."

Russert is America's most overrated journalist (Wolf Blitzer's a close second). He failed to challenge Administration flacks in the lead up to Iraq, and then he joined the drumbeat for war with Iran. Russert doesn't have the guts to take on anybody with real power, and so he takes cheap shots at easy marks like Dennis Kucinich and Shirley MacLaine.

The alternative debate was a historic victory against corporate censorship but it generated huge bills that cleaned out the campaign's reserve cash. Mike's absence from the debates also made it impossible to maintain even his modest fundraising levels. In contemporary politics, if people don't see you on TV, you might as well not be running. Whoever made the decision to kick Gravel out of the debate ultimately killed the campaign.

CONCLUSION
AMERICA'S WISE FOOLS

> KENT: *This is not altogether fool, my lord.*
>
> FOOL: *No, faith, lords and great men will not let me; if I had a monopoly out, they would have part on't:*
>
> *King Lear,* Act I Scene IV

In a Shakespearean tragedy, only the fools are allowed to speak truth to power. The same seems to be the case in today's America where the most visible critics of the political and media elite are comedians Jon Stewart and Stephen Colbert. As with Shakespeare's jesters, there is much wisdom to learn from these wise fools.

Jon Stewart Versus the Echo Chamber

Every night on the *Daily Show,* Jon Stewart mocks both the politicians and the media that covers them. He often strings together video clips of various news shows pushing a single storyline that has no basis in reality. "They poke fun at how cheesy the regular news shows are, and somebody needs to do that," said *Daily*

Show fan Joe Van Vleet, a twenty-five-year-old college student.

Nicole Vernon, a twenty-four-year-old bartender, said she finds much of television news "silly." She said, "[Stewart] keeps it very truthful and straightforward."

A 2004 Pew Research Center poll found that twenty-one percent of people aged eighteen to twenty-nine cited the *Daily Show* as a place where they regularly learned presidential campaign news. By contrast, twenty-three percent of the young people identified ABC, CBS, or NBC's nightly news broadcasts as their news source. The *Daily Show* reached a ratings milestone during the two weeks of the 2004 Iowa caucus, New Hampshire primary, and the State of the Union address when it attracted more male viewers aged eighteen to thirty-four than any of the network evening news shows. Responding to the Pew Study, a *CBS Evening News* producer sighed, "I've passed being depressed about that."[3]

In an entertaining way, Stewart nurtures in his young audiences a cynical approach to the media's storylines. Our educational system should do the same.

Media Studies Education

For decades, high school civics courses have taught our kids how the system of government works. It's time to teach them how the political media operates. We need more citizens who understand how the storyline gets created and how it shapes "the news." Just as we teach students literary criticism, we also should teach them to approach visual images with a critical eye. Social Studies teachers should take a cue from Jon Stewart and examine video clips of past presidential speeches and old political commercials. They should generate class discussions about the images and get students to think about how politicians communicate ideas and manipulate voters. Students must learn about the nature of the echo chamber so that they can critically wade through media frenzies and not get swept up in the hype.

Stephen Colbert vs. the White House Correspondents

Stephen Colbert once described the character he plays on his *Colbert Report* as "a fool who has spent a lot of his life playing not the fool." In true Shakespearian style, Colbert's fool spoke the truth to the king's face at the 2006 White House correspondents' dinner, an annual event that displays the clubby relationship between White House and the national media.

The spectacle of the press corps yukking-it-up with the president has always been painful to watch. But the White House correspondents' dinner reached a new low in 2004 when George Bush treated the audience to a slide show of him searching for Iraq's WMDs under Oval Office furniture. "Those weapons of mass destruction gotta be somewhere.... Nope, no weapons over there.... Maybe under here." With each slide, laughter erupted from the audience that included the thoroughly amused Joe Lieberman and Nancy Pelosi, along with esteemed members of the press. Nothing could have displayed the callousness of the Washington elite more fully then those cheap guffaws. What kind of human beings could find humor in the biggest intelligence failure in American history that was currently killing thousands of Americans and Iraqis? Of course, why not laugh? No one in the press or the government lost his or her job over the horrible WMD mistake. Furthermore, most journalists and congressmen in the room were as responsible as George Bush for hyping Saddam's nonexistent threat. Best to just let bygones be bygones.

Two years and 20,000 Iraqi deaths later, Stephen Colbert challenged the backslapping mirth of the White House correspondents' dinner by taking on Bush and the media. Playing his faux right-wing persona, Colbert stood a few feet from Bush and declared, "I stand by this man. I stand by this man because he stands for things. Not only *for* things, he stands *on* things, things like aircraft carriers and rubble and recently flooded city squares. And that sends a strong message, that no matter what happens to America, she will always rebound with the most powerfully staged photo-ops in the world."

Bush aides and supporters began leaving before Colbert finished. "Colbert crossed the line," one top Bush aide complained.

Another recalled the look on Bush's face as he sat within spitting distance of Colbert, "I've been there before, and I can see that he is [angry]. He's got that look that he's ready to blow."

Colbert then turned his searing soliloquy on the media. "Over the last five years, you people were so good over tax cuts, WMD intelligence, the effect of global warming. We Americans didn't want to know, and you had the courtesy not to try to find out. Those were good times, as far as we knew." Colbert took a shot at the unwritten rules of the echo chamber, "Let's review the rules. Here's how it works. The president makes decisions. He's the decider. The press secretary announces those decisions, and you people of the press type those decisions down. Make, announce, type. Just put 'em through a spell check and go home. Get to know your family again. Make love to your wife. Write that novel you got kicking around in your head. You know, the one about the intrepid Washington reporter with the courage to stand up to the Administration? You know, fiction!"

Colbert's blistering performance hit so close to home that reporters and news producers filtered out any reference to him in their coverage of the dinner. Instead, their storyline focused on a lame skit involving President Bush and his impersonator Steve Bridges making light of Bush's malapropisms and mispronunciations.

On ABC's *This Week,* George Stephanopoulos played an excerpt of Bush and Bridge's act and remarked that the dinner "gets more inventive every year." Stephanopoulous did not even mention Colbert. On NBC's *Sunday Today,* co-host Lester Holt showed clips of the Bush-Bridges routine observing that the "relationship between the White House press corps and the president can be a contentious one, but last night it was all laughs." NBC's *Nightly News* also chose to air footage of Bush's performance, and they too ignored Colbert, as did CNN and the three major networks on their morning shows.[4]

New York Times White House correspondent Elisabeth Bumiller filed a report, "A New Set of Bush

Twins Appear at Annual Correspondents' Dinner," detailing Bush and Bridge's routine and provided some background on how the new Bush twins rehearsed. The article noted, "With his approval ratings in the mid 30s and a White House beset by troubles, there is some evidence that Mr. Bush worked harder on his performance this year than in the past." Bumiller also failed to mention Colbert.[5] But that is not surprising. Bumiller admitted to coddling Bush and being "very deferential" to him during the White House press conference right before the Iraq War. She, like the rest of her colleagues in the press corps, chickened out because, in her words, "It's live, it's very intense, it's frightening to stand up there. Think about it, you're standing up on prime-time live TV asking the President of the United States a question when the country's about to go to war. There was a very serious, somber tone that evening, and no one wanted to get into an argument with the president at this very serious time."[6]

No one was expecting Bumiller and her fellow correspondents to "get into an argument" with the president. The public just needs the White House press corps to ask some challenging questions. If Bumiller and her colleagues had half the guts of Stephen Colbert, they might have done their jobs. No wonder they all ignored or downplayed Colbert's performance. He made them look like a bunch of fools.

The *Washington Post* got particularly indignant that a jester would turn his wit against the Beltway court. The *Post* report on the event, "The New Bush Twins: Double Dubya," intoned, "The reviews from the White House Correspondents' Association Dinner are in, and the consensus is that President Bush and Bush impersonator Steve Bridges stole Saturday's show, and Comedy Central host Stephen Colbert's cutting satire fell flat because he ignored the cardinal rule of Washington humor: Make fun of yourself, not the other guy."[7] Actually, the cardinal rule of Washington humor is don't mention Washington hypocrisy.

On MSNBC, *Time* magazine's Michael Allen told Chris Matthews that Colbert "went over about as well as David Letterman at the Oscars." Matthews followed up by asking, "Why do you think he was so bad?" On *Countdown*, Keith Olbermann asked *Washington Post* political columnist Dana Milbank, "Was this the right tone at the right venue? Was there a line crossed here in some way?"[8] Milbank responded, "I don't think he really crossed the line. I just think he wasn't terribly funny. And he had the misfortune of following Bush, who actually did put on one of the *better performances* of his presidency." Milbank added, "So I think [Bush] probably comes out ahead in this whole thing." In previous years, the echo chamber would have been able to drown out Colbert's insurrectionary monologue with silence or a dismissive storyline, but times had changed.

Citizen Journalism

A blog called Crooks and Liars was one of the first places to host the video and not only recorded their busiest day on record, but Nielsen BuzzMetrics also ranked their Colbert post as the second most popular blog post for all of 2006. *Editor and Publisher*'s and Salon.com's extensive coverage of the Colbert speech drew record numbers of viewers to their websites. Clips of Colbert's comic tribute climbed to the number one, two, and three spots atop YouTube's "Most Viewed" video list.[9]

In an unprecedented move for the network, C-SPAN demanded that YouTube and iFilm remove the video from their sites. But before YouTube caved, the various clips of Colbert's speech were viewed 2.7 million times in less than forty-eight hours. Google Video shrewdly purchased the exclusive rights to carry the video, and it remained near the top of

Google's most popular videos for the next two weeks. A website called "Thank You Stephen Colbert" logged almost 50,000 "Thank You's" within its first five days of existence.

Chicago Sun-Times TV Critic Doug Elfman credited the Internet with saving Colbert's speech from being lost in the echo chamber, "Internet stables for liberals like the behemoth dailykos.com began rumbling as soon as the correspondents' dinner was reported in the mainstream press with scant word of Colbert's combustive address."[10]

Having seen the unfiltered performance on C-SPAN or YouTube, bloggers began offering a much different take on the event than the embarrassed media was peddling. Seventy thousand articles were posted to blogs about Colbert's performance on the Thursday after the event, the most of any topic.[11]

Writing for the *Huffington Post,* playwright Christopher Durang pointed out, "The media's ignoring Colbert's effect at the White House Correspondents' Dinner is a very clear example of what others have called the media's penchant for buying into the conservative/right-wing narrative [storyline]. In this instance, the narrative is that President Bush, for all his missteps, has a darling sense of humor and is a real regular guy, able to poke delightful fun at himself and his penchant for mis-using and mispronouncing words."

"Who cares if he lied to start a war?" Durang asked, "Or chose to ignore all contrary opinion, which, as far as war-starting goes, is pretty crummy. Who cares if he declares he's above the law, and according to the *Boston Globe*, yesterday there are something like 750 laws he's decided don't apply to him as Commander in Chief? ...Colbert's was a brave and shocking performance," Durang declared, "and for the media to pretend it isn't newsworthy is a total bafflement. And a symbol of how shoddy and suspect the media is."[12]

Christopher Durang is a playwright and an actor, but like thousands of non-journalists, he uses the power of the Internet to break old media's monopoly on information and opinion. Blogging and YouTube have opened up the doors to citizen journalists who will play a vital role in saving our nation from the echo chamber's attempts to stifle inconvenient truths.

Nothing has done more to expose the discrepancies between news coverage and reality than the Internet. Everyday, citizen journalists and online media critics, like Crooks and Liars and Media Matters, critique the mainstream media news accounts. Bloggers play a key role in democratizing the news media and bringing transparency to everything from shoddy commercial products to sham charities. We must teach our kids to join this information revolution by becoming citizen journalists. They should be taught in school how to hunt down information and discriminate between good and bad sources. They should learn how to write clear, digestible blog posts. Just as we encourage budding citizens to vote, we must also teach young people to take an active approach to media.

Participatory Journalism

In the 1960s, new left radicals criticized representative democracy because the people surrendered their power to elected officials who made the decisions. Sixties radicals called for *participatory democracy* that would actively involve the people in governmental decision-making. Today, war and economic crises have plunged our country into mire similar to the Vietnam era. We need to confront these challenges with *participatory journalism* that will empower ordinary Americans to search for news, share it, and engage in online political debate. If there is one lesson we have learned over the last several years, it's that we cannot trust the mainstream media to give us accurate information. The people must become active in their news consumption in order to check the power of the echo chamber and save our democracy.

Chapter One: The Real 9/11 Cover-up

1. Remarks by the President at Connecticut Republican Committee Luncheon, Greenwich, Connecticut, 9 April 2002.

2. Quoted in Jim Neilson, "Fertilizing Bush: Growing a Great Leader for Difficult Times," *Cultural Logic,* 2004.

3. Jim Neilson, "Fertilizing Bush: Growing a Great Leader for Difficult Times."

4. Michael Elliot, "We Will Not Fail," *Time,* 1 October 2001; Jim Hoagland, "Putting Doubts to Rest," *Washington Post,* 23 September 2001, B7; Jeffrey Birnbaum, "The Making of a President," *Fortune,* 12 November 2001; *CBS Sunday Morning,* 9 December 2001; Kenneth T. Walsh, "I Will Not Yield. I Will Not Rest," *U.S. News & World Report,* 23 September 2001; Martha Brant, "West Wing Story: Behind a Great Speech," *Newsweek,* 26 September 2001; Quoted in Jim Neilson, "Fertilizing Bush: Growing a Great Leader for Difficult Times."

5. Martha Brant, "West Wing Story: Behind a Great Speech."

6. Card quoted in Walsh, "I Will Not Yield." Card quoted in Brant, "West Wing Story: Behind a Great Speech." Massimo Calabresi, et al., "Life on the Home Front," *Time* (online) http://www.time.com/time/covers/1101011001/story3.html, 2001.

7. Jim Neilson, "Fertilizing Bush: Growing a Great Leader for Difficult Times"; Jeffrey Birnbaum, "The Making of a President"; Howard Fineman, "A President Finds His True Voice," *Newsweek,* 24 September 2001; James Klurfeld, "From the Rubble, Politician Bush Emerges as Presidential Leader," *Newsday,* 27 September 2001; James Carney and John F. Dickerson, "A Work In Progress," *Time,* 22 October 2001.

8. Quoted in Jim Neilson, "Fertilizing Bush: Growing a Great Leader for Difficult Times"; Judy Keen, "Same President, Different Man in Office," *USA Today,* 29 October 2001; Richard Berke, "Jokes Remain, But Many Say Bush Is Showing Signs of War's Burden," *New York Times,* 8 December 2001; Brian Williams, *The News with Brian Williams,* CNBC, 28 December 2001; Howard Fineman and Martha Brant, "This Is Our Life Now," *Newsweek,* 3 December 2001; Patrick E. Tyler and Elizabeth Bumiller, "Bush Offers Taliban 2nd Chance," *New York Times,* 12 October 2001.

9. "Bush Finds His Gravitas," *Christian Science Monitor,* 25 September 2001, 8; Doyle McManus, "President Finds Voice, Leadership in Terrorism Crisis," *Los Angeles Times,* 19 September 2001; Michael Duffy, *Washington Week in Review,* 28 December 2001; David Gregory, *The News with Brian Williams,* CNBC, 28 December 2001; Quoted in Jim Neilson, "Fertilizing Bush: Growing a Great Leader for Difficult Times."

10. Jeffrey Birnbaum, "The Making"; Michael Elliott, "We Will Not Fail," *Time,* 1 October 2001, 18; Judy Keen, "Strain of Iraq War Showing on Bush, Those Who Know Him Say," *USA Today,* 2 April 2003; Walsh, "I Will Not Yield," *U.S. News & World Report,* 1 October 2001; Fineman and Brant, "This Is Our Life Now"; McKinnon quoted in Richard L. Berke, "A Nation Challenged: The President; Jokes Remain, But Many Say Bush Is Showing Signs of War's Burden."

11. Quoted in Jim Neilson, "Fertilizing Bush: Growing a Great Leader for Difficult Times."

12. Jeffrey Birnbaum "The Making"; Ronald Brownstein, "Bush's Success Partly Lies in His Measured Response," *Los Angeles Times*, 10 December 2001; Margaret Carlson, "Unleash the Pitcher Within," *Time*, 12 November 2001.

13. "Mr. Bush's New Gravitas," *New York Times*, 12 October 2001.

14. Rather quoted in Robert Jensen, "Dan Rather and the Problem with Patriotism," *Global Media Journal*, Fall 2003; "Dan Rather: Mainstream Media Are Frightened and Timid," *The Memory Hole*, 21 January 2003.

15. Quoted in Jim Neilson, "Fertilizing Bush: Growing a Great Leader for Difficult Times."

16. The *Panama City News Herald* memo is cited in Joe Davidson, "Dependant upon Accuracy and Fairness," Poynteronline (http://www.poynter.org/content/content_view.asp?id=4667), 18 December 2001; "Bill Moyers Interviews Greg Mitchell," *Now with Bill Moyers*, (http://www.pbs.org/now/transcript/transcript_mitchell.html).

17. Amanpour and Briganti quoted in Peter Johnson, "Media Mix," *USA Today*, 14 September 2003.

Chapter Two: War Drums Pounding in the Echo Chamber

1. William Rivers Pitt and Scott Ritter, *War on Iraq*, Context Books, 2002, 52.

2. Bob Woodward, *Plan of Attack*, Simon and Schuster, 2004.

3. Barton Gellman and Walter Pincus, "Depiction of Threat Outgrew Supporting Evidence," *Washington Post*, 10 August 2003.

4. Howard Kurz, "In the Hot Seat: Tim Russert on His Ego, His Bias, His Father Worship and What He Really Thinks About Tax Cuts," *Washington Post,* 23 May 2004.

5. Dana Milbank, "An Ex-Aide's Testimony, A Spin Through VP's PR," *Washington Post,* 26 January 2007.

6. James Risen, "Threats and Responses: The View from Prague: Prague Discounts an Iraqi Meeting," *New York Times,* 21 October 2002.

7. Frank Rich, *The Greatest Story Ever Sold: The Decline and Fall of Truth from 9/11 to Katrina,* Penguin Press HC, New York, 2006.

8. Rich at 68.

9. According to a *Washington Post* poll taken in August 2003, 69 percent of Americans believed Hussein had a role in the 9/11 attacks (Dana Millbank and Claudea Deane, "Hussein Link to 9/11 Lingers in Many Minds," *Washington Post,* 6 September 2003).

10. Michael Moss, "Pentagon Study Links Fatalities to Body Armor," *New York Times,* 7 January 2006.

11. Judith Miller, "Iraqi Tells of Renovations at Sites for Chemical and Nuclear Arms," *New York Times,* 20 December 2001.

12. Judith Miller, "Iraqi Tells of Renovations at Sites for Chemical and Nuclear Arms," *New York Times,* 20 December 2001.

13. James Bamford, "The Man Who Sold the War," *Rolling Stone,* 17 November 2005.

14. Michael Gordon and Judith Miller, "US Says Hussein Intensifies Quest for A-Bomb Parts," *New York Times,* 8 September, 2002.

15. Barton Gellman and Walter Pincus, "Depiction of Threat Outgrew Supporting Evidence," *Washington Post,* 10 August 2003.

16. Id.

17. Quoted in Christopher Bollyn, "Media Coverage of Iraq Called 'Shameful,'" http://www.AmericanFreePress.net, 12 April 2004.

18. Doyle McManus, "Global and National Security," LA World Affairs Council, C-SPAN, 23 January 2003.

19. Judith Miller, "Verification Is Difficult at Best, Say the Experts, and Maybe Impossible," *New York Times,* 18 September 2002.

20. Judith Miller, "C.I.A. Hunts Iraq Tie to Soviet Smallpox," *New York Times,* 3 December 2002.

21. Judith Miller, "Defectors Bolster U.S. Case Against Iraq, Officials Say," *New York Times,* 24 January 2003.

22. Quoted in Rich at 74.

23. Michael Massing, "Now They Tell Us," *The New York Review of Books,* 26 February 2004; Howard Kurtz, "The Post on WMDs: An Inside Story Prewar Articles Questioning Threat Often Didn't Make Front Page," *Washington Post,* 12 August 2004.

24. Howard Kurtz, "The Post on WMDs: An Inside Story Prewar Articles Questioning Threat Often Didn't Make Front Page," *Washington Post,* 12 August 2004.

25. *Media Matters,* "*Washington Post* Buried Report Questioning Iran Nuke Intel, Despite Mea Culpa for Doing the Same on Iraq," 18 September 2006.

Chapter Three: Lipstick on a Pig: The Iraq War Coverage

1. Christopher Bollyn, "Media Coverage of Iraq Called 'Shameful,'" http://www.AmericanFreePress.net, 12 April 2004.

2. "Report: Bush Talked of Bombing Al-Jazeera," *Associated Press,* 22 November 2005; Jeremy Schaill, "Did Bush Really Want to Bomb Al Jazeera?," *The Nation,* 23

November 2005.

3. Interview with Gay Talese, David Shankbone, *Wikinews,* October 27, 2007.

4. Alessandra Stanley, "A Nation at War: The TV Watch; Networks Make the Most of their Frontline Access," *New York Times,* 21 March 2003.

5. Id.

6. Steve Rendall and Tara Broughel, "Amplifying Officials, Squelching Dissent," *FAIR,* May/June 2003.

7. Id.

8. Rich at 80.

9. Susan Schmidt and Vernon Loeb, "'She Was Fighting to the Death' Details Emerging of W. Va. Soldier's Capture and Rescue," *Washington Post,* 3 April 2003.

10. John Kampfner, "Saving Private Lynch Story Flawed," BBC News, 15 May 2003.

11. Lynda Hurst, "Jessica Lynch's Story Is Turning 'into a Monster' for the Bush Administration," *Toronto Star,* 16 November 2003.

12. Quoted in *Source Watch* on Jessica Lynch.

13. David Zucchino, "Army Stage-Managed Fall of Hussein Statue," *Los Angeles Times,* 3 July 2004.

14. Jon Wiener, "The Saddam Statue-Toppling, Four Years Later," *The Nation,* 12 April 2007.

15. Id.

16. Robin Andersen, "That's Militainment! The Pentagon's Media-Friendly 'Reality' War," *Fairness and Accuracy in Reporting,* May/June 2003

17. UPI, 9 April 2003.

18. Rich at 89.

19. Rich at 91.

20. *Lou Dobbs Tonight,* CNN, 1 May 2003.

21. Matthews quoted in "Mission Accomplished: A Look Back at the Media's Fawning Coverage of Bush's Premature Declaration of Victory in Iraq," *Media Matters*, 27 April 2006.

22. Judith Miller, "After Effects: Prohibited Weapons, Illicit Arms Kept Till Eve of War, An Iraqi Scientist Is Said to Assert," *New York Times*, 21 April 2003.

23. Charles Layton, "Miller Brouhaha," *American Journalism Review*, August/September 2003

Chapter Four: Ahmadinejad: America's Next Top Bogeyman

1. Nazila Fathi and Joel Brinkley, "U.S. Pursuing Reports that Link Iranian to Embassy Seizure in '79," *New York Times*, 1 July 2005.

2. Brian Knowlton, "Iranians Deny Leader Is Tied to Hostage Standoff," *International Herald Tribune*, 30 June 2005.

3. Brian Knowlton, "Iranians Deny Leader Is Tied to Hostage Standoff."

4. "Former Hostages Allege Iran's New President Was Captor, Takeover Leader: Ahmadinejad 'Absolutely' Not Involved," http://www.CNN.com, 30 June 2005.

5. Nazila Fathi and Joel Brinkley, "U.S. Pursuing Reports that Link Iranian to Embassy Seizure in '79."

6. Joseph Kahn, "China's Costly Quest for Energy Control," *New York Times*, 27 June 2005.

7. Michael Gordon, "'CATASTROPHIC SUCCESS' The Strategy to Secure Iraq Did Not Foresee a 2nd War," *New York Times*, 19 October 2004.

8. Scott Shane, "Panel Rebukes C.I.A. and F.B.I. for Shortcomings in Overhaul," *New York Times*, 16 April 2005.

9. Christopher Dickey, "Iran's Nuclear Lies: Iran Says Its Nuclear Program Is for Peaceful Uses Only. But a History of Deception Raises Doubts," *Newsweek*, 11 July 2005.

10. Ali Akba Dareini, "Iran Expands Uranium Enrichment Effort," Associated Press, 10 April 2007.

11. Id; Joshua Holland, "Media Obscures Iran's Nuclear Program with 'Fog Facts,'" AlterNet.org, 10 April 2007.

12. All poll numbers from PollingReport.com.

13. James Gordon Meek and Alison Gendar, "President of Iran Requests Tour of Ground Zero on N.Y. trip," *Daily News,* 21 September 2007.

14. Id.

15. Murray Weiss and David Seifman, "NYC Denies Ahmadinejad Request to Tour Ground Zero," *New York Post,* 19 September 2007.

16. Bobby Gosh, "Ahmadinejad Ground Zero Ploy," *Time,* 20 September 2007.

17. David Saltonstall, Oren Yaniv and Allison Gendar, "Columbia University Ripped for Inviting Iranian Thug," *Daily News,* 21 September 2007.

18. Id.

19. Newt Gingrich Interview with John Gibson, Fox News, 24 September 2007.

20. Jeffrey Steinberg, "Behind the Annapolis Meeting and the Iran NIE Shock," *Executive Intelligence Review,* 14 December 2007.

21. Id.

22. Gareth Porter, "Cheney Tried to Stifle Dissent in Iran NIE," *IPS,* 10 February 2008.

Chapter Five: The "Likeability" Election

1. *Choosing the President 2008,* The Lyons Press, Guilford, CT, 52.

2. John Dickerson, "Barackwater," http://www.Slate.com, 14 December 2006.

3. Kenneth Lovell, "Barack's Fairy Tale Ballistic Bubba Blasts Obama," *New York Post,* 9 January 2008.

4. Lynn Sweet, "Obama's Rezko Problem Spills Over," *Chicago Tribune,* 26 January 2008.

5. Thomas Edsall, "As Iowa Nears, Clinton Allies Quietly Raise Obama's Cocaine Use," *Huffington Post,* 11 December 2007.

6. Alec MacGillis, "Clinton N.H. Official Warns Obama Will Be Attacked on Drug Use," 12 December 2007.

7. Matt Taibbi, "Mike Huckabee, Our Favorite Right-Wing Nut Job," *Rolling Stone,* November 2007.

8. Hillary Clinton at Take Back America Conference, Washington, DC, 6 June 2007.

9. http://news.aol.com/newsbloggers/2007/04/22/the-associated-press-pulls-an-ann-coulter-on-john-edwards/.

10. Mark Leibovich, "In New Hampshire, Bill Clinton Finds Less Spark," *New York Times,* 7 January 2008.

11. Frank Rich, "Haven't We Heard This Voice Before?" *New York Times,* 13 January 2008.

12. Benedict Carey, "The Crying Game, and the Political Herd," *New York Times,* 13 January 2008.

Chapter Six: Maverick in the Echo Chamber

1. Kerry Eleveld, "Mike Gravel's Big Splash," *Advocate,* 3 July 2007.

2. "Gravel Pissed Over HRC Diss," Queerty.com, 11 July 2007.

Conclusion: America's Wise Fools

1. "Young America's News Source: Jon Stewart," http://www.CNN.com, 2 March 2004.

2. "Media Touted Bush's Routine at Correspondents' Dinner, Ignored Colbert's Skewering," *Media Matters,* 1 May 2006.

3. Elisabeth Bumiller, "A New Set of Bush Twins Appear at Annual Correspondents' Dinner," *New York Times,* 1 May 2006.

4. Elisabeth Bumiller quoted in "A White House Farewell Letter," http://www.Salon.com, 5 June 2006.

5. Amy Argetsinger and Roxanne Roberts, "The New Bush Twins: Double Dubya," *New York Times,* 2 May 2006.

6. Alex Koppelman, "Lou Dobbs, Stephen Colbert and the Myth of the Liberal Media," http://www.Salon.com, 3 May 2006.

7. "Stephen Colbert at the 2006 White House Correspondents' Association Dinner," www.Wikipedia.org

8. Id.

9. Id.

10. "Chris Durang, "Ignoring Colbert, Part Two," *Huffington Post,* 1 May 2006.